Chambers

Pocket Guide to Language of Music

D1431183

Also published by Chambers

Chambers Pocket Guide to Music Forms & Styles

Other Chambers Pocket Guides

Chambers Pocket Guide to Good English
Chambers Pocket Guide to Good Spelling
Chambers Pocket Guide to Phrasal Verbs

Chambers
Pocket Guide to Language of Music

Wendy Munro

Chambers

© 1987 W & R Chambers Ltd Edinburgh

Reprinted 1988, 1991

British Library Cataloguing in Publication Data

Munro, Wendy
  Pocket guide to language of music.
  — (Chambers pocket guides).
  1. Music—Terminology
  I. Title
  781′.23   ML108

ISBN 0-550-18032-X

Typeset by Blackwood Pillans & Wilson Ltd.

Printed and bound in Great Britain by Cox & Wyman Ltd.

PREFACE

Language of Music is compiled in an A to Z form to help you interpret the most commonly found musical terms in scores, academic musical analysis and general discussion. It is also designed to enable you to enjoy and appreciate the style, form, texture, mood and technical expertise central to a composition or performance. You will find that many expressive musical terms are in Italian since the custom of inserting indications of speed and force began in Italy in the 17th century, and as Italian music was widely popular, so the Italian terms were cultivated. In the 18th century Couperin and Telemann introduced French and German terms and, since Schumann in the 19th century, the practice of inserting terms in the composer's native language has become common. You will find, therefore, terms from many different languages in this pocket guide.

Easy to use and easy to understand, *Language of Music* presents each headword in bold type, e.g. **allegro**; other commonly used phrases related to the headword are in *italics*. Italics are also used for titles of works. Within the entries there may be other terms in bold type which indicates that you can look up more information under that particular word. There are no abbreviations apart from those commonly found in musical scores, e.g. **vc** or **vla** which are listed alphabetically, and there are examples in the book of notated examples of ornaments, key and time signatures and other common musical symbols.

Language of Music is written to assist professional, amateur, performing and passive musicians alike in their quest to understand and appreciate music to the full. Many pleasurable hours have been spent compiling this dictionary, and I hope you will gain as a result more insight into this fascinating subject.

Wendy Munro

List of Abbreviations

Am.	American
Brit.	British
Eng.	English
Fr.	French
Gael.	Gaelic
Ger.	German
Gk.	Greek
Hung.	Hungarian
It.	Italian
Lat.	Latin
Pol.	Polish
Port.	Portuguese
Sp.	Spanish

A

A
    Note of the scale commonly used for tuning the orchestra. Also an analytical term for the first section of a piece.

a, à (It., Fr.)
    At, by, for, with, in, to, e.g. *a tempo* (It., 'in time').

ab (Ger.)
    Off, away.

abbandono (It.)
    A free, impassioned style.

abbassare (It.)
    To lower, tune down.

abbellimenti (It.)
    Ornaments.

abdämpfen (Ger.)
    To mute.

abend (Ger.)
    Evening.

abendlied (Ger.)
    Evening song.

aber (Ger.)
    But.

abgesang (Ger., 'aftersong')
The concluding section of a stanza of a Minnesinger or Meistersinger song.

abnehmend (Ger.)
See **diminuendo**.

absolute music
Music composed simply as music, with no references to emotions, stories, paintings or any other non-musical subject.

absolute pitch
Perfect pitch. The ability to recognise or recall any note

abstossen (Ger.)
To play **staccato**.

abstract music
Same as **absolute music**.

a cappella (It.)
In the church style. This term is used of unaccompanied church choral music.

accarezzevole (It.)
Caressing.

accelerando (It.)
Getting gradually quicker.

accent
Stress or pressure in the rhythm of music or a particular beat.

accento (It.)
Accent.

acciaccatura (It.)
A crushed dissonant note of the shortest possible duration played before or after the main note or chord and immediately released.

accidental
> A sharp, double sharp, flat, double flat or natural prefixed to a note. An accidental refers only to the bar in which it occurs.

accompaniment
> Subordinate part(s) added to principal instrument(s) music.

achtel (Ger.)
> Quaver.

acoustics
> (1) The science of sound. (2) The sound properties of a building, etc.

act tune
> A piece played between the scenes of an English 17th-century theatrical work. The modern term is **entr'acte.**

acute
> An **ornament** in 17th-century English music.

acute mixture
> An organ stop giving **overtones** tuned slightly sharp.

adagietto (It.)
> Slightly faster than **adagio.**

adagio (It.)
> Slow and broad. Also used to describe a slow movement.

adagissimo (It.)
> Very slow.

added sixth
> The major sixth added to a major or minor **triad.** In C major, A is added above the triad of C E G. Used greatly in jazz.

à deux cordes (Fr.), **a due corde** (It.)
> On two strings.

ad lib
> (1) Freedom as to rhythm, tempo. (2) Improvisation. (3) Inclusion or omission of a passage.

a due

a due (It.)
In two parts.

aeolian mode
A **mode** which, on the piano, uses the white notes from A to A.

affettuoso (It.)
With feeling.

affrettando (It.)
Becoming faster and more agitated.

agitato (It.)
Restless and wild.

agogic
Used of deviations from the strict tempo and rhythm necessary for the subtle performance of a musical phrase.

agréments (Fr.)
See **ornaments.**

air
A simple tune for voice or instrument.

alberti bass
A keyboard moving figuration for the left hand using simple **arpeggio** treatment of a series of chords. This was much used by 18th- and early 19th-century composers.

alborada (Sp.)
Morning song.

aleatoric music
Music containing chance or random elements. A trend since 1945 with composers like John Cage and Karlheinz Stockhausen.

al fine (It.)
To the end.

alla (It.)
To the, at the, in the manner of.

alla breve (It.)

Take the **minim** as the main unit, *not* the **crotchet**, e.g. 2/2 instead of 4/4.

allargando (It.)

Getting broader.

alla turca (It.)

In the Turkish style.

alla zingarese (It.)

In the style of gypsy music.

alla zoppa (It.)

Syncopated.

allegretto (It.)

Slower than **allegro**.

allegro (It.)

Lively and rather fast.

allemande (Fr.)

(1) A moderately slow dance movement often opening the baroque suite in 4/4 time. (2) A brisk dance in triple time current in the late 18th and early 19th centuries. A prototype of the waltz.

alt

The phrase *in alt* in the vocal sense applies to notes from G above the treble stave to F above that. The notes in the octave above are *in altissimo*.

alto

(1) The highest male voice employing falsetto. (2) A low female voice (contralto). (3) French for viola. (4) The prefix to an instrument indicating one size larger, e.g. alto saxophone. (5) The alto clef from which the viola plays and where middle C is on the third line.

alto clef

amore (It.)
Love. *Con amore*, lovingly.

amoroso (It.)
Lovingly.

ancora (It.)
Still, yet.

andante (It.)
At a moderate speed.

andantino (It.)
Slightly faster than **andante**.

anglaise (Fr.)
Short for *danse anglaise*. An English dance in quick duple time
introduced into the suite in the 17th century.

anglican chant
A type of harmonised melody used for psalm singing in the
Church of England.

animato (It.)
Lively.

answer
A responding musical phrase particularly in a **fugue.** A *real
answer* occurs when the answer exactly reproduces the **subject**
(entry or theme) a fifth above or a fourth below. A *tonal answer* is
the subject reproduced, but this time slightly modified so as to
keep within a certain key.

anthem
(1) A short solemn vocal composition used in Church of England
services. (2) A short patriotic vocal composition.

anticipation
The sounding of a note or notes before the chord to which it or
they belong.

antiphon (Gk.)

The plainsong setting of sacred words sung as responses in Roman Catholic or Greek orthodox services. The term *antiphonal* derives from the practice of alternating performances between sets of singers stationed apart.

a piacere (It.)

At pleasure.

appassionato (It.)

Impassioned.

appoggiatura (It.)

A musical **ornament** (chiefly 18th century) of an auxiliary note falling or rising to a harmonised note. It can be written or unwritten.

a punta d'arco (It.)

With the point of the bow.

arabesque (Fr. and Eng.), **arabeske** (Ger.)

A short piece with decorative qualities.

arco (It.)

Play with the bow.

aria (It.)

Air or song for one or more voices now used exclusively of solo song in opera and oratorio. A *da capo aria* is one in which the first section is finally repeated after a contrasting section.

arietta (It.)

A little or light aria.

arioso (It.)

Similar to an **aria**, i.e. not **recitative**.

arpeggio (It.)

A chord performed with the notes separated.

arrangement
    A harmonised setting for voices or instruments of an existing melody.

ars antiqua (Lat.)
    Western European medieval music based on plainsong (see **plainchant**) and **organum**.

ars nova (Lat., 'the new art')
    Breaking away from **ars antiqua** and introducing duple time and much independence of part-writing.

assai (It.)
    Very. *Allegro assai*, very quick.

atonal
    Not in any key.

attacca (It.)
    Go on to the next section without a repeat.

augmentation
    The lengthening (usually doubling) of the time-values of notes in a melody, e.g. in fugues.

augmented interval
    The increased version of another interval, e.g. an *augmented first* is C to C sharp.

augmented sixth chord
    This has three forms: (1) *Italian*, A flat, C, and F sharp. (2) *French*, A flat, C,D and F sharp. (3) *German* A flat, C, E flat and F sharp.

augmented triad
    A chord composed of two major thirds, e.g. C, E and G sharp.

ayre
    A song for one or several voices in 17th-century England.

B

B

Note of the scale. Also an analytical term for the second section of a piece.

badinage or **badinerie** (Fr., 'playfulness')

This term was used as a title-movement in quick 2/4 time in the 18th-century suite, e.g. Bach's *Suite in B minor* for flute and strings.

bagatelle (Fr., 'trifle')

Usually a short and light piano piece. Beethoven wrote 26, e.g. *Für Elise*.

ballabile (It.)

In a dancing style.

ballad

A traditional solo song telling a story with music repeated for each verse. In the 19th century the term came to mean a rather sentimental drawing-room song. However, it may also be applied to a self-contained narrative song, e.g. Schubert's *Erlkönig* or to operatic arias, e.g. *Senta's Song* from *The Flying Dutchman* by Wagner. It describes a sentimental song in jazz.

ballade

Chopin's term for a long, dramatic piano piece suggesting narrative. *The Four Ballades* by Chopin are inspired by the poems of Mickiewicz. Grieg, Liszt and others later used the title.

ballet

Dancing of Italian origin established at the French court in the 16th century and used by Lully in operas. Nowadays it is generally conceived as using orchestral music (sometimes specially composed) and stage decoration. In Britain it generally describes any piece of serious and lengthy stage dancing. **Opera-ballet** gave almost equal importance to opera and ballet in 17th- and 18th-century France, but it may also describe some modern ballets with singing, e.g. Prokoviev's *Cinderella*.

ballett (Eng.), **balletto** (It.)
A vocal composition similar to the **madrigal** and popular in England and Italy around 1600. Characteristics are a dance-like nature and the singing of *fa la la* as a refrain. Also called *fa-la*.

ballo (It.)
A dance. *Tempo di ballo*, in dance time.

band
An instrumental ensemble, e.g. brass band or jazz band. Originally, the term was applied to any large-scale instrumental group.

bar
The metrical division of music marked by vertical bar-lines drawn across a **staff** or staves, between which are certain numbers of beats. Hence, 2, 3 or, as in the example below, 4 beats to the bar. The American name for bar is 'measure'. A double bar (two vertical lines close together) indicates the end of a piece, or section.

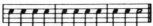

bar.
Abbreviation of **baritone**.

barber-shop songs
Sentimental songs sung by amateur male quartets in close harmony.

barcarolle (Fr. from It.)
A song or instrumental associated with the Venetian gondoliers in 6/8 or 12/8 swaying time, e.g. the barcarolle in *The Tales of Hoffman* by Offenbach.

baritone

Male voice between bass and tenor with a range of two octaves from G (on bottom line bass clef) to G (above middle C). The term is also a prefix for instruments indicating the range below the tenor type, e.g. baritone saxophone.

baroque (Port., *barroco* 'rough pearl')

The musical period approximately between 1600 and 1750 encompassing composers such as Monteverdi, Frescobaldi and Gabrieli (early baroque) and Bach and Handel (late baroque).

bass

(1) Lowest male voice with a range from E below bass clef to E above middle C. (2) Lowest note or part in a chord, composition, etc. (3) Prefixed to an instrument, the term indicates the largest or second largest member, e.g. bass clarinet. (4) Abbreviation for double bass. (5) Bass clef.

bass clef

bass-baritone

Male baritone voice with a strong upper register.

basse chiffrée (Fr.)

See **figured bass**.

basso (It., 'bass')

Basso cantante describes a lyrical singing voice; *basso continuo* is the same as **continuo** and *basso ostinato* is the same as **ground bass**.

battuta (It., 'beat')

A battuta, in strict time; *senza battuta*, with no regular pulse; *ritmo di tre battute*, accent falls at the beginning of every three beats.

bel canto (It.)

Fine, sustained singing in the Italian manner with emphasis on beauty of tone and agility.

ben, bene (It.)

Well, very.

berceuse (Fr., 'bercer' to rock)
An instrumental cradle song or lullaby in compound duple time, eg Chopin's *Berceuse* for piano.

bergamasque (Fr.), **bergamasca** (It.), **bergomask** (Eng.)
A peasant's dance from Bergamo, north Italy, with 2 beats to the bar. Composers have used the term in titles, e.g. Debussy's *Suite Bergamasque* for piano.

bestimmt (Ger.)
Decisively.

beweglich (Ger.)
Agile.

bewegt (Ger.)
With animation. *Bewegter*, faster. *Mässig bewegt*, at a moderate speed.

binary form
A composition in two balanced sections. After beginning in the tonic, the first section modulates to the dominant or other related key. The second section, opening in the new key, then moves back to the original key. If the original key is a minor one, then the first section ends with the relative major. Compositions in binary form are mostly short. Developed into compound binary form or **sonata form**.

bis (Fr., 'twice')
Used in French when the English use **encore**.

bisbigliando (It., 'whispering')
Harp technique of repeating notes softly and quickly.

bitonality
A 20th-century concept of using two keys simultaneously, evident in Stravinsky's music.

bocca chiusa (It.)
Singing with closed lips.

bogen (Ger.)
Instruction to bow for string players. See also **arco**.

bolero (Sp.)

A Spanish dance similar to the **cachucha** performed to the dancers' singing with castanets in simple triple time.

bouche fermée (Fr.)

Singing with closed lips.

bourrée (Fr.)

A popular dance of the 18th and 19th centuries, often found in dance suites. Beginning with an upbeat, it is fast-moving, with two main beats to the bar.

bowing

The marking for stringed instruments to show which notes should be played down-bow and which up-bow.

down bow ⊓   *up bow* ∨

brace

The line with bracket joining two staves in piano music.

bravo (It.)

Brave, fine. An interjection expressing approval.

bravura (It.)

A display of a musical passage requiring great virtuosity by the performer.

break

(1) A short solo passage in jazz. (2) The change of tone quality between registers on voice or instruments. (3) The verb describing the deepening of the male voice in puberty.

breit (Ger.)

Grandly, broadly. Used to describe the manner not the tempo of a performance.

breve

Originally this meant the shortest note in early written music. When short notes were introduced and long ones discarded, the breve became the longest note. It is equivalent to two semibreves. See table on page 123.

brevis (Lat.)
Short.

brillant (Fr.), **brillante** (It.)
Brilliant. Usually a direction for solo performers.

brindisi (It.)
Toast or drinking song.

brisé (Fr., 'broken')
The use of **arpeggio** in keyboard and harp music and of **detaché** bowing in string music.

broken chord
A chord in which notes are sounded one after the other, not simultaneously.

broken octaves
Alternate notes played an octave apart. Used in piano writing.

btb
German abbreviation of normal orchestral bass tuba in F.

buffo, buffa (It., 'comic')
Opera buffa, comic opera. The noun also means comic actor or singer.

burden, burthen
Refrain line (sometimes nonsense) at the end of a ballad verse.

C

C
Note of the scale.

cabaletta (It.)
(1) A simple and short aria often repeated with reiterated rhythms. (2) A final quick but elaborate section of an aria or duet as used by Verdi, made up of several sections. (3) A type of song in rondo form. (4) A recurring passage in a song varied on each repeat.

cachucha
A lively Andalusian dance in 3/4 time for solo performer. Similar to **bolero**.

cadence
A closing musical sentence, e.g. the ending of a composition, phrase or section. This closing effect is achieved by certain chord progressions. The most common are:
perfect cadence, (dominant to tonic) sounding complete.
plagal cadence, (subdominant to tonic) sounding 'amen'.
imperfect cadence, (tonic or other chord to dominant) sounding 'unfinished'.
interrupted cadence, (dominant to submedient) surprise key, sounding 'minor' if in major key and major if in minor key.
feminine cadence, resolving on a weaker beat than its predecessor.
Phrygian cadence, ending on the dominant of the relative minor, e.g. in C major, the final chord would be E G sharp and B.

cadenza (It.)
A solo vocal or instrumental passage before the final cadence, generally occurring in the first movement in the classical **concerto.** It suggests improvisation of the main themes and a

'showing-off' of the player's virtuosity. However, Mozart and other composers since have written out their cadenzas in full.

calando (It.)
Getting weaker and slower.

calypso
A song from Trinidad having a syncopated rhythm often with topical or satirical words. Accompanied by primitive instruments.

cambiata
See **nota cambiata**.

camera, da (It.)
For the room. See also **sonata**.

camerata (It., 'society')
The artistic group which was responsible for the origin of opera around 1600 in Florence. Members included Caccini and Peri.

can can
A lusty Parisian dance in quick 2/4 time involving high kicking. Used by Offenbach in *Orpheus in the Underworld* (1881) and still performed in the cabarets of Paris.

cancrizans
Crab-wise. The back-to-front order of notes otherwise described as 'retrograde motion'. A *canon cancrizans* is a canon in which an imitating voice states the initial theme notes in reverse order.

canon
A contrapuntal work in which a melody, stated by one part is repeated by one or more voices in turn, each entering before the previous part has finished. This results in overlapping. Simple canons include the round and catch. Various forms exist:
canon at the unison, the voice enters at the same pitch as the previous one.
canon at the fifth, the imitating voice enters a fifth higher.
double canon, two simultaneous canons, each for 2 voices.
accompanied canon, a canon with other performing voices or instruments not taking part in the canon.

perpetual canon, A never-ending canon, when each voice ends, it begins again. Others include canon by **augmentation, diminution** and **inversion** in which themes are treated in any of these ways.

cantabile (It.)
In a singing style.

cantata (It.)
Generally a vocal composition with instrumental accompaniment telling a story by means of arias and recitatives. In the 17th and 18th centuries two types existed: *cantata da camera* which was secular and *cantata da chiesa* which was suitable for church. Writers of this period included Schütz and J.S. Bach who made the cantata more theatrical with the use of choruses, chorales and strings. In the 19th century the term described short narrative choral works accompanied by full-scale orchestra with arias, recitatives and soloists. Modern writers include Bartók, Stravinsky and Britten.

cantatrice (It.)
Female singer.

canticle
(1) A bible hymn (not a psalm) used in Christian liturgy. (2) A concert composition usually of religious text much favoured by Britten.

cantilena (It.)
(1) A smooth lyrical melody line. (2) A vocal part in choral writing carrying the main theme (3) a type of vocal exercise (*solfeggio*).

canto (It.)
A song or melody. *Marcato il canto*, bring out the melody.

cantus (Lat.)
A song or melody. *Cantus firmus*, 'fixed song', i.e. an existing melody borrowed from religious or secular sources by 14th–17th-century composers for setting to other melodies which are in counterpoint against it. In the 16th century the term describes the highest voice-line in a choir.

canzona (It., 'song')

(1) A medieval Italian poem set to music. (2) A short, fairly polyphonic instrumental piece popular in the 16th and 17th centuries. (3) *Canzoni* in the 18th century described short arias and likewise short lyrical instrumental pieces.

canzonet

Originally a shorter type of canzona but it also describes a type of **madrigal** and a simple solo song not from an opera.

cappella (It., 'chapel')

A cappella, alla cappella, in the church style, i.e. unaccompanied choral music.

capriccio (It.), **caprice** (Fr.)

Generally applied to short, light and lively pieces. In the 17th century the term described keyboard works in bright, fugal style. In the 19th century it described piano pieces in rhapsodic style, e.g. by Brahms.

carmen (Lat.)

Song.

carol

A seasonal religious song, now most commonly associated with Christmas. The singing from door to door originated in the mid-19th century.

cassation

An 18th-century composition in simple divertimento style, i.e. an orchestral or chamber work in several short movements, e.g. by Mozart.

castrato (It.)

Adult male singer with soprano or contralto voice.

catch

A type of **round** of amusing sometimes bawdy character, e.g. by Purcell.

cavatina (It.)

(1) An operatic song in one section and of regular form. (2) A

short and slow lyrical instrumental movement, e.g. the theme from *The Deer Hunter* originally composed by Raff for violin and piano.

cédez (Fr.)
Go a little slower.

celere (It.)
Quick. *Celeramente*, quickly.

chaconne (Fr.)
A vocal or instrumental composition in slow, stately three-beat time with a **ground bass.** Popular in the 17th century in keyboard music and operas.

chaleur (Fr.)
Warmth.

chamber music
Generally, instrumental music suitable for a small venue, e.g. a room as opposed to a large church or theatre. Therefore, the music is of a more intimate nature, with a limited number of performers, one player per part. Nowadays much chamber music is played in concert halls.

chamber orchestra
A small orchestra suitable for playing in a room or other small venue.

chamber opera
Opera with reduced forces, i.e. a small orchestra and a few singers suitable for an intimate theatre, not an immense opera house.

chamber sonata or **sonata da camera** (It.)
A type of suite prevalent in the 17th and 18th centuries mainly in the form of dance movements for two or more stringed instruments with keyboard accompaniment.

chanson (Fr.)
Song. Also like **air** applied to an instrumental piece of vocal character.

chant

Usually music which is sung in accordance with ritual or tradition, e.g. unaccompanied vocal music in Christian services like the ambrosian or gregorian chant (plainsong). The term is also used in the Anglican church for psalm and canticle singing.

chest voice

Vocal lower register as opposed to 'head voice', the higher register.

chiaro, chiara (It.)

Clear.

chiesa, da (It.)

For the church, unlike the secular *da camera* for the room. See also **sonata.**

choir

(1) A body of singers. (2) The part of a church where singers are seated. (3) Short for choir organ (4) The American term for an orchestral section, e.g. *brass choir*.

chorale

A Lutheran metrical hymn-tune, e.g. *Ein' feste Burg*, much used by J.S. Bach. A *chorale-prelude* is an instrumental piece based on a chorale, usually for organ.

choral symphony

(1) A symphony using a chorus. (2) A work of symphonic proportions but scored for voices only.

chord

The simultaneous sounding of two or more notes.

chorus

A large body of singers with several voices to each part. The term also indicates the refrain of a song.

chromatic

Intervals outside of the diatonic scales (i.e. major or minor) notated by the use of **accidentals.** A chromatic chord is one which contains notes foreign to the key. Chromaticism is a feature of romantic music.

classical music

Music after the **baroque** era between 1750 and 1830, written by composers such as Haydn and Mozart, who produced and refined the symphony, concerto and string quartet. Classical music was followed by romantic music.

clef

The symbol to determine the location of notes on the **staff**, placed normally at the beginning of each line, or other point where the new clef cancels the old. There are many clefs, e.g. treble, bass, alto and tenor.

close

An American term for **cadence**. A *half-close* is an imperfect cadence and a *full-close* is a perfect cadence.

close harmony

Harmony in which notes of chords are written closely together, e.g. in barber-shop quartets.

cluster

A 20th-century concept of playing a group of adjacent notes simultaneously on the piano, e.g. with the forearm or a piece of wood. The American term is *tone-cluster* and the British term is *note-cluster*. Pioneered by Cowell in 1912 and used by Ives.

coda (It.,'tail')

The concluding section at the end of a movement, not usually of structural necessity. However, Beethoven's codas have great significance in his musical design.

codetta (It., 'little tail')

Similar to **coda** but on a smaller scale, i.e. 'rounding off' a section of a movement as opposed to a whole movement.

coloratura (It.)

Agile and florid style of vocal performance.

come (It.)

Like. *Come prima*, as at first. *Come sopra*, as above.

common chord

A major or minor triad in root position, e.g. in C major, the common chord is C E G.

common time

Four crotchets to the bar, written 4/4 or C.

comodo (It.)

Easy, easily-flowing, leisurely.

compound time

Any beat-unit divisible into three, e.g. 6/8, 9/8, 12/8. Opposite of *simple time*.

con (It.)

With. *Cogli, coi, col, coll', colla, colle*, with the.

concert

The public performance of music other than opera, ceremony or religious service. A performance by one or two is a *recital*.

concertante

(1) A work for orchestra or for two or more instruments with prominent solo parts. (2) The *sinfonia-concertante* is a work with a form nearer to a **symphony** than concerto but employing solo instruments and orchestra.

concerted

An adjective applied to a performance by several people of a work in which all parts are more or less equal.

concertino

(1) A little and light **concerto**. (2) The soloist group in the 17th- and 18th-century **concerto grosso**. (3) A less formally structured work than a concerto for one or more solo instruments with orchestra.

concerto

(1) A large-scale work, generally in three movements involving solo instrument(s) contrasted with orchestra and standardised by Mozart. Also called *solo concerto*. (2) An orchestral work in several contrasting movements with or without solo instruments, often supported by **figured bass** in the 17th and 18th centuries.

concerto grosso (It., 'great concerto')

(1) An orchestral work involving interplay between the *ripieno* or *concerto* (main body of instruments) and the *concertino* (small group of solo instruments) each with its own **continuo.** Prevalent in the 17th and 18th centuries and written by Bach, Handel. (2) A 20th-century description for certain works based on 17th- and 18th-century ideas.

concert overture

A one-movement orchestral work written as an independent concert piece usually having a title influenced by the arts or emotions, e.g. Mendelssohn's *The Hebrides*.

concord

Pleasing to the ear and sounding harmonically resolved. However, interpretations of this term vary considerably. The opposite is *discord*.

concrete music

See **musique concrète**.

conduct

To direct a performance of either singers, players or both with a baton or hands in order to give precise indications of dynamics, phrasing and speed.

conductus

A medieval secular vocal composition having a *cantus firmus* to which other parts were added in close harmony. The *cantus firmus*, or given part, was either already in existence or specially composed.

consecutive intervals

Harmonic intervals of the same kind, e.g. thirds succeeding one another in the same parts. A consecutive fifth would be C with G played above, followed by D played with A above. *Hidden fifths* are implied consecutive fifths.

conservatoire (Fr.) or **conservatory**

A school for musical training.

consonance

Same as **concord**.

consort

An old English word for a group of instruments or chamber ensemble. *Whole consort* applies to one family of instruments and *broken consort* applies to mixed families.

continuo (It.)

Abbreviation of *basso continuo*. Same as **figured bass.**

contra (It.), **contre** (Fr.), **kontra** (Ger.)

Prefixes indicating an instrument lower in pitch, usually an octave lower, e.g. contrabass trombone.

contralto

The lower type of female voice having a range from F below middle C to G above the treble clef.

contrapuntal

Adjective from **counterpoint.**

coperto (It., 'covered')

E.g., drums, which may be muffled with a cloth to give a muted effect.

corda, corde

String(s). In piano playing, *una corda* (one string) indicates the use of the soft pedal. The terms *tre corde* or *tutte le corde* cancel this, indicating the release of the soft pedal.

counterpoint

The sounding together of two or more separate parts of rhythmic and melodic independence, in harmony. Part B is described as being the counterpoint or 'in counterpoint' to A, etc. *Invertible counterpoint* occurs when any one melody strand can exchange its position for another, e.g. the bass becomes treble. Between two parts, this is called *double counterpoint*.

counter-tenor

A rare male voice higher than a tenor, current in the 17th century and revived in the 20th century. Also called male alto. See **falsetto.**

coup d'archet (Fr.)

Stroke of the bow, the attack with the bow.

courante (Fr.)

A lively dance in triple time popular in the baroque period and found in the **suite**.

crescendo (It.)

Getting gradually louder. Shown

cross relation or **false relation**

(1) The sounding together in one chord of a note and its chromatic alteration, e.g. A natural and A flat. (2) The progression where a note in a chord, e.g. A natural, is followed by its chromatic alteration, A flat, in another part of the next chord.

crotchet

Equivalent to half a minim or two quavers. The American term is *quarter note*. See table on page 123.

csárdás (Hung.)

Hungarian dance in contrasting sections: *lassù* (slow) and *friss* (quick).

cycle

(1) A set of works, especially songs, intended to be performed as a group with thematic connection, e.g. Schubert's song cycle *Die Winterreise*. (2) The cycle of fifths: a chain of perfect fifths which will lead back to the original note (at a different octave) after working through the other eleven notes of the chromatic scale. It is useful for learning key signatures.

cyclic form

A work in which a theme connects more than one movement. Beethoven introduced it into symphonic music (e.g. in his *Fifth* symphony) and romantic composers developed it further.

D

D

Note of the scale.

da (It., 'from')

Da capo or *DC*, repeat from the beginning. *Da capo al fine*, repeat up to the word *fine*. *Da capo al segno*, repeat to the sign.
Dal segno, repeat from the sign.

damping pedal

Piano soft pedal.

danse (Fr.), **danza** (It. and Sp.)

Dance.

decrescendo (It.)

Becoming softer. Shown

degree

Position of note in scale, e.g. D is the second degree in the scale of C major.

dehors (Fr., 'outside')

To be played prominently, i.e. bringing out a certain melody or part.

descant

(1) In modern general sense, it is the additional part sung above a given melody, e.g. in a hymn or folksong. Occasionally the descant can be improvised. (2) The medieval note-against-note style of **organum**, usually called *discant* and written in contrary motion.

desk
> Two orchestral performers sharing a music stand.

détaché (Fr.)
> Detached, staccato. *Grand détaché*, staccato with full bow for each note. *Petit détaché*, staccato played with point of the bow.

development
> The section of a movement when initial statements of themes are expanded, developed, modified and broken up.

diaphony (Gk.)
> Describes types of **organum** admitting dissonance.

diatonic
> Adjective describing major and minor scales and also modes. The opposite of chromatic music which introduces notes not in the prevailing key. Diatonic harmonies, intervals, passages, etc. are made up, therefore, with notes of the key of the moment.

diction
> Clear and correct enunciation in singing.

dim
> Abbreviation of (1) **diminuendo**, (2) **diminished** (in dance-band harmony, etc.).

diminished intervals
> A perfect or minor interval reduced by a semitone, in practice only pertaining to the diminished fifth (semitone less than a perfect fifth) and the diminished seventh (a semitone less than a minor seventh).

diminished triad
> A triad in which the perfect fifth is reduced chromatically by a semitone, e.g. C E and F sharp.

diminuendo (It.)
> Gradually becoming softer. See **decrescendo**.

diminution
> The treatment of a melody by shortening the time-values of notes, usually by half, e.g. in fugues and canons.

discant
    See **descant**.

discord
    See **concord**.

dissonance
    Same as **discord** (see **concord**).

div
    Abbreviation of **divisi**.

diversions
    Alternative name for **variations**.

divertimento (It.)
    Chiefly an 18th-century term for an entertaining suite of movements for chamber ensemble or orchestra. Mozart wrote in this style.

divertissement (Fr., 'amusement')
    (1) Entertainment in ballet form, sometimes with songs, found in operas or plays for contrast, e.g. the operas of Lully. (2) Same as **divertimento**. (3) Instrumental piece or **fantasia** employing popular tunes.

divisi (It., 'divided')
    Score instruction for instrumentalists (usually string players) performing two-part or double-note passages indicating the division into two groups instead of all playing both notes.

dodecaphonic music
    Alternative term for **serial music**.

dolce (It.)
    Sweet and gentle. *Dolcissimo*, very sweetly.

dolente (It.)
    Sorrowful.

dominant
    The fifth note of the major or minor scale, e.g. G is the dominant of C major. Therefore, the dominant chord of C major is G B D,

and the dominant seventh chord (with the addition of the seventh note from the bass, i.e. G) is G B D F. The *secondary dominant*, which is the dominant of the dominant in C major, would be D (i.e. fifth note up from G).

dopo (It.)
   After.

doppio (It.)
   Double. *Doppio movimento*, at double the speed of the preceding section.

dorian mode
   The mode represented by white keys on the piano beginning on D, with dominant A and final D.

double
   (1) Prefixed to an instrument, e.g. 'double bassoon', it may either mean that it is (a) an octave lower than the ordinary bassoon or (b) that it combines the features, in the case of the 'double horn', of the horn in F and horn in B flat. (2) The 18th-century term for variation or ornamental repeat of the main theme, e.g. in a dance movement.

double bar
   Two bar lines placed closely together to signify the end of the composition or section. Often preceded or followed by repeat signs, i.e. dots.

double counterpoint
   Invertible **counterpoint** in two parts occurring frequently in fugues.

double flat
   A prefix to a note indicating pitch to be lowered by two semitones. On the keyboard B double flat is A.

double sharp
   Prefix x attached to note indicating pitch to be raised by two semitones. On the keyboard F double sharp is G.

double stop
   A two-note chord produced on a bowed string instrument by using two adjacent strings. Also includes chords where open string is used.

double tonguing
   The rapid playing of notes (often repeated ones) on flute or brass instruments produced by articulating alternately consonants T and K. Not possible on reed instruments.

douce(ment) (Fr.)
   Sweet (sweetly), gentle (gently).

down-beat
   The downward movement of the conductor's stick or hand indicating the first beat of the bar. The term, therefore, can also mean the first beat of the bar.

down-bow
   The pulling of the bow across a stringed instrument. The *up-bow* is the pushing of the bow in the opposite direction.

dramma per musica (It.)
   Title used in 17th- and 18th-century Italy for **opera**.

drängend (Ger.)
   Hurrying.

dringend (Ger.)
   Urgent.

drohend (Ger.)
   Threatening.

due corde (It.)
   Two strings. (1) In piano music this occasionally indicates the release of the soft pedal. (2) In violin music this indicates that the passage playable on one string is to be played on two.

duet
   A composition for two performers sometimes with an accompaniment. A piano duet is for two pianists.

duettino (It.)
A little duet.

duetto (It.)
Duet.

duo
Same as duet but mainly an instrumental composition for two performers (with the exception of the piano duet).

duodecuple
Same as dodecaphonic, which is the alternative name for **serial** or twelve-note music.

duple time
Time in which the number of beats in the bar is divisible by two or four, e.g. 2/4, 4/4, 2/2. Time with four beats per bar is also known as *common* or *quadruple* time. If beats in the bar are divisible by two, e.g. 2/4, then it is *simple duple time*. If beats are divisible by three, e.g. 6/8 it is *compound duple time*.

duplet
A pair of notes occupying time usually taken by three, e.g. 6/8 or 3/8.

dynamics
The degrees of softness or loudness in music indicated by signs or words on the score.

E

E
Note of the scale.

éclatant (Fr.)
(1) Brilliant, bright. (2) Blaring.

écossaise (Fr.)
Short for *danse écossaise*. Although meaning Scottish dance, the term is apparently not of Scottish origin. A quick dance in 2/4 time, it was popular in Britain and on the Continent in the late 18th and early 19th centuries. Cultivated by Beethoven.

eilen (Ger.)
To hurry. *Nicht eilen*, do not hurry.

einfach (Ger.)
Simply.

eisteddfod (Welsh, 'assembly')
Music or competition festival. The important National Eisteddfod is held in Wales.

elegy
Song or instrumental composition for the dead.

embellishments
Same as **ornaments**.

embouchure (Fr.)
Also known as *lip*. The correct position of lips to the mouthpiece of an instrument to produce accurate intonation and good tone. The term also refers to the mouthpiece of a wind instrument.

empfindung (Ger.)

Feeling. *Mit empfindung*, with feeling.

enchaînez (Fr.)

Link together, i.e. go straight on to the next section or movement without a break.

encore (Fr.)

Again. This term, however, is only used in English to mean 'perform it again'. French term is *bis*.

enharmonic

Describes the difference in notation between, e.g. F natural and E sharp. On fixed-note instruments, e.g. piano, there is no change of pitch and on other instruments, or the voice, there is only a small change to adjust to the new harmony. Therefore, 'enharmonic change' describes the changed notes of the performer's part from, e.g. D sharp to E flat and *enharmonic modulation* describes whole chords with changed notation.

ensemble (Fr., 'together')

(1) A group of performers, e.g. a vocal ensemble, which would not be as big as a choir. (2) In opera, an ensemble is an item for several soloists with or without chorus.

entr'acte (Fr.)

(1) Interval during a play or opera. (2) Music to be played between the acts of a play or opera.

entrée (Fr.)

Chiefly a 17th-century French music term for (1) an introductory piece for the entry of characters in ballet or opera; (2) an independent instrumental piece of similar nature; (3) the equivalent of a scene or act in ballet or opera.

entry

(1) The entrance of a theme in a **fugue** occurring not only at the beginning but also at later stages in the composition. (2) A 17th-century term for a **prelude**.

episode

(1) In a **rondo** this represents a contrasting section between

recurrences of the main theme. (2) In a **fugue** it is a section linking (by means of contrast, modulation or possibly using subject material) one entry and another. In both contexts, an episode has a subordinate role.

episodical form
Same as **rondo** form.

equale (Old It., 'equal')
Piece or pieces (*equali*) for instruments of the same kind.

equal voices
Voices of the same range, e.g. sopranos, or the same kind, e.g. all female.

espressivo (It.)
With expression.

essential note
A note forming part of a chord, e.g. E in the chord of C major, C E G, as opposed to a **passing note** or **appoggiatura**, etc.

estampie (Fr.)
A popular dance form in the 13th and 14th centuries consisting of several sections (*puncta*) each of which has a first ending (*ouvert*) and a second ending (*clos*).

estinto (It., 'extinct')
Music to be played so that it is barely audible.

étouffez (Fr., 'damp')
Indication to harp or cymbal players, etc that sound must be immediately cut short.

étude (Fr., 'study')
An instrumental piece to improve or demonstrate certain technical points. However, many, e.g. by Chopin, have much artistic merit.

etwas (Ger.)
Rather, somewhat.

exercise

(1) An instrumental or vocal piece intended to improve aspects of technique and of no artistic value. (2) The term for a keyboard suite in the 18th century. (3) A composition required by candidates for university and college degrees.

exposition

The initial statement of a musical theme or idea upon which a movement or piece is based. In **fugue**, the exposition is the initial statement of the subject to each voice in turn. The exposition is completed when each voice has been heard for the first time. In **sonata form**, it is a repeated section in which the main themes are first stated before moving on to the development section.

expressionism

A 20th-century term borrowed from painting and applied to other art forms implying a reaction against impressionism (e.g. the works of composers such as Debussy). Musically it is especially applied to the works of Schönberg, Berg and some compositions of Hindemith.

expression marks

Indications on the score provided by the composer to aid accurate performance of a work and consisting of dynamics (i.e. degrees of loudness and softness), tempo and mood.

extemporisation

Same as **improvisation**.

F

F
Note of the scale.

f
Abbreviation of **forte**.

f clef
Another name for **bass** clef.

faburden or **fauxbourdon**
Literally this term means 'false drone'. Originally this described a method of improvising parallel harmony below a plainsong melody. In modern use the term means (1) a four-part harmonisation of a hymn with the tune in the tenor or (2) a descant added above a hymn-tune sung by the congregation.

facile (Fr. and It.)
Easy, fluent. *Facilmente*, easily or fluently.

fado (Port.)
A type of Portuguese folk song in **binary form** with four beats to the bar; the tempo may be fast or slow.

fa-la
Same as *balletto* or *ballett*.

false relation
Same as **cross relation**.

falsetto (It.)
Singing or speech by an adult male voice in a higher register than normal. It is sometimes employed as a comic effect and is used by tenors for notes lying above their range.

fandango (Sp.)
A lively Spanish dance in 3/4 or 6/8 time accompanied by guitar, castanets and performers' singing. The fandango includes sudden stops and speed increases.

fanfare
(1) A flourish for trumpets (or other imitating instruments) usually for an introduction or proclamation. (2) French for brass band.

fantasia (It.), **fantaisie** (Fr.), **fantasie** (Ger.), **fantasy** (Eng.)
This style is generally associated with the abandoning of set rules for free flights of the composer's imagination. Specific definitions include: (1) a romantic mood piece of the 19th century, e.g. by Schumann; (2) a contrapuntal piece, in several sections for one or many players, current in the 16th and 17th centuries, of improvisatory nature, with 'fancy' as an alternative name. The title *phantasy* was used for the 20th-century revival of the form. The terms *free fantasy* or *free fantasia* are synonyms for **development**, e.g. in **sonata form**.

fantasiestück (Ger.)
A short piece similar to **capriccio** or **intermezzo**.

farandole (Fr.)
A dance of Provence in 6/8 time accompanied by pipe and tabor.

fausset (Fr.)
Falsetto.

feierlich (Ger.)
Solemn.

feminine cadence
The final chord of a cadence occurring on the weak beat of the bar, instead of the more usual strong beat.

fermata (It.)
Pause.

ff
Abbreviation of **fortissimo**.

figure
> A short musical phrase (not as long as a theme) which is recognisable through repetition in a composition.

figured bass or **basso continuo** (It.)
> The bass part (played on keyboard or other chordal instrument) with figures written below the notes indicating the harmonies to be played above them. This system was used greatly in the baroque period as an accompaniment for soloists or to enrich the general texture of a larger composition.

final
> The note on which the melody ends in church **modes**. In *authentic* modes , the final is on the tonic. In *plagal* modes, it falls on the fourth degree of the scale.

finale (It.)
> Final. In English there are two main meanings: (1) the last movement of a work in several movements; (2) the lengthy concluding section of an **opera**, often subdivided into smaller sections with contrasting tempos or keys. Involves several singers and often a chorus.

fine (It.)
> End. This term sometimes occurs in the middle of music, often where there is an instruction to repeat an opening section. The direction *fine* indicates the end of a piece.

fino al segno (It.)
> As far as the sign.

fioritura (It., 'a flowering')
> Decoration of a melody with **ornaments** which may be notated or improvised. Evident in 17th- and 18th-century Italian opera.

first movement form
> Occasionally used as an alternative name for **sonata form**.

flamenco or **cante flamenco** (Sp.)
> An Andalusian song performed with guitar accompaniment and dancing of a mostly sad nature. Various types of flamenco exist and are named after districts, e.g. malagueña and sevillana.

Flamenco-style guitar employs quite different and forceful techniques compared to classical guitar playing.

flat

A lowering in pitch which may be a semitone, or a description of someone singing or playing flat unintentionally. A *double flat* indicates a lowering of the pitch by two semitones. See table on page 125 for notation.

flebile (It.)

Mournful.

fliessend (Ger.)

Flowing.

flourish

(1) Fanfare. (2) Decorative musical figuration notated or improvised.

flutter-tongue

Extremely fast articulation of sound on a wind instrument by the tongue, like trilling. On the flute the resulting tone is pigeon-like.

forte (It.)

Loud. Abbreviated *f*.

fortissimo (It.)

Very loud. Abbreviated *ff*.

forza (It.)

Force. *Con forza*, with force, vigorously.

forzando (It.)

Strongly accented. Abbreviated *fz*.

foxtrot

Originally an American dance in duple time of which there are two main types—fast and slow. It first became popular in 1912.

frottola (It.)

A popular and light Italian strophic song for several voices, with the melody on top, flourishing around 1500. Particularly heard in aristocratic circles.

fuga
(1) (Lat.) A **canon** in the 15th and 16th centuries. (2) (It.) A **fugue**.

fugato
Describes a section of a composition in fugal style which is not actually a **fugue**.

fuge (Ger.)
Fugue.

fughetta (It.)
Short **fugue**.

fugue
A contrapuntal composition for two or more voices or parts built around a theme, which is successively imitated by entries of each voice at the beginning and developed throughout the piece. The initial entry in the **tonic** key is called the *subject*. The second entry in the **dominant** is called the *answer*. If this answer is exact (i.e. it reproduces the subject note for note in the dominant) then it is a *real answer*. If the answer is slightly modified to preserve tonality, it is called a *tonal answer*. After having announced the subject or answer, each voice passes on to another thematic element known as the *countersubject*. After each voice has made its initial entry the *exposition* or first section of the fugue is complete. Thereafter, further entries of the subject appear, separated by contrapuntal *episodes* and the subject may be treated by **augmentation**, **diminution**, **inversion**, etc. J.S. Bach was one of the great masters of the fugue.

full anthem
An Anglican church anthem sung by a full choir throughout, with no soloists.

full close
Alternative name for **perfect cadence**.

fundamental
First or lowest note of the harmonic series.

funebre (It.), **funèbre** (Fr.)
Funeral. *March funèbre*, funeral march.

fuoco (It.)

Fire. *Con fuoco*, with fire.

furiant

A quick Czech dance in triple time with syncopated rhythms.

futurism

A movement (around 1909) involving Italian writer Marinetti and composer Rossolo who employed 'noise instruments' in music like whistlers, thunderers, exploders, etc. The movement lasted until the 1920s in Italy and was a reflection of the mechanical world.

fz

Abbreviation of **forzando**.

G

G
Note of the scale.

gaillard (Fr.)
Same as **galliard**.

gaio, gaia (It.)
Gay.

galant (Fr. and Ger.), **style galant**
Courtly. This term, adopted by German writers, refers to a mid-18th-century style characterised by a homophonic, formal elegance as opposed to the German contrapuntal traditional style. This was practised by C.P.E. Bach and influenced Mozart.

galantieren (Ger.)
Optional dances, e.g. **polonaise** or **minuet**, in the 18th-century suite, normally placed between the **sarabande** and **gigue**.

galliard
A lively dance usually in triple time often contrasted (although often thematically linked) with the slower **pavan** which it followed.

galop
A quick 19th-century ballroom dance in 2/4 time.

gamba (It.)
Abbreviation for *viola da gamba*.

garbato (It.)
Graceful.

gavotte
A fairly quick dance in 4/4 time usually beginning on the third beat of the bar.

gebrauchmusik (Ger.)
Same as **utility music**.

gedämpft (Ger.)
Muted.

gehalten (Ger.)
Sustained. *Gut gehalten*, well sustained.

gehend (Ger.)
At a moderate speed.

geistlich (Ger.)
Sacred.

gemessen (Ger.)
Held back, tempo sustained.

gemütlich (Ger.)
Easy-going, cosy, comfortable.

general pause
Complete silence. A rest of at least one bar for the whole orchestra. Abbreviation is GP.

German sixth
A type of 'augmented sixth' chord, e.g. A flat, C, E flat and F sharp which also may be treated as a dominant seventh chord (in this case in the key of D flat).

gesangvoll (Ger.)
Songful.

geschleift (Ger.)
Smooth. Same as **legato**.

geschwind (Ger.)
Quick.

gestossen (Ger.)
Detached. Same as **staccato**.

getragen (Ger.)
Slow and sustained. Same as **sostenuto**.

giga
See **gigue**.

gigue or **giga** (It.), **jig**
A lively dance in **binary form**, usually in 6/8 or 12/8 time. Often occurs as the last movement in the 18th-century dance suite.

giocoso (It.)
Merry, playful.

giusto (It.)
(1) In strict time. (2) At a reasonable speed.

glee
A simple and short part-song in several sections for male voices, flourishing in Britain between 1650 and 1830.

glissando
The sliding up or down a scale, often abbreviated by *gliss.* or a wavy or straight stroke between the highest and lowest note.

GP
Abbreviation of **general pause**.

grace-note
Same as **ornament**, used to embellish a melody line and normally printed in smaller type.

gradevole (It.)
Pleasing.

grandezza (It.)
Grandeur. *Con grandezza*, with grandeur.

grandioso (It.)
In an imposing manner.

grand opera

A vague term describing: (1) the serious, entirely sung operas as opposed to the lighter **opéra-comique** which had dialogue; (2) operas on a grand and lavish scale.

grave (It.)

Slow and solemn.

gregorian chant

A type of **plainsong** associated with Pope Gregory I (590–604) existing as a large collection of ancient monophonic melodies which were until quite recently used in the Roman Catholic Church.

ground bass or **basso ostinato** (It.)

A bass line or pattern repeated over and over while upper parts proceed. The ground bass is a foundation for varied melodic, contrapuntal or harmonic treatment. Forms which use this device include the **chaconne** and **passacaglia**.

gut (Ger.)

Markedly.

gymel (Lat. *gemellus*, 'twin')

A type of two-part late medieval English vocal music, with great use of thirds and sixths.

H

habanera (Sp.)
A syncopated Cuban dance introduced into Spain in the 19th century with singing, usually in 2/4 time.

halb(e) (Ger.)
Half. *Halbsopran*, mezzo-soprano. *Halbtenor*, baritone.

half-close
An **imperfect cadence**.

half-note
An American term for minim. See table on page 123.

harmonic series
A set of notes produced by a vibrating string or air column, determining the difference of tone-colours of instruments.

harmony
The sounding of notes together which is musically significant. The main unit of harmony is the chord, which may be inverted and is based on the major scale. The chords are built around the degrees of the scale. In C major, for example, the *tonic* chord consists of C E G also called I, the *supertonic* of D F A (II), the *mediant* of E G B (III), the *subdominant* of F A C (IV), the *dominant* of G B D (V), the *submediant* of A C E (VI) and the *leading note* chord of B D F (VII). The primary chords in a composition are I, IV and V, around which most popular music is based. Many rules on modulation, chromaticism and discords exist in traditional harmony writing.

head voice
Upper register of voice.

heiter (Ger.)
Cheerful.

heptachord
The scale of seven notes, e.g. the modern major or minor scale.

hidden fifths
Consecutive fifths implied, but not actually present in harmony and nevertheless frowned upon by academics.

hocket
In medieval church music, the insertion of rests into vocal parts for expressive purposes.

homophony (Gk., 'same-sounding')
Music in which parts move together presenting a top melody with accompanying chords. The opposite of **polyphony**.

hondo or **cante hondo** (Sp.)
A sad Andalusian song employing some intervals smaller than a semitone.

hornpipe
A lively English dance, in triple time in the early 16th century. From the mid 18th-century onwards it was in 4/4 time, acquiring an association with sailors.

humoresque (Fr.), **humoreske** (Ger.)
An instrumental composition of a capricious nature. Schumann wrote in this style.

hymn
A Christian song of praise sung by a congregation with words specially written.

I

idée fixe (Fr., 'fixed idea')
Berlioz' term for **motto theme** which means a recurring theme in a composition used, e.g. in his *Symphonie Fantastique*

idyll
A literary term for a work of pastoral or peaceful nature and transferred to music, e.g. *Siegfried Idyll* by Wagner.

illustrative music
Descriptive music evoking a poem, novel, play, painting emotion or other non-musical source. More common term is **programme music**.

imitation
A device in part-writing in which one voice repeats (or approximately repeats) a musical figure previously stated by another voice. **Canon** and **fugue** employ imitation with strict rules.

imperfect cadence
See **cadence**.

impressionism
Term borrowed from painting, describing the works of Monet, Degas, etc. and transferred to music referring to the atmospheric music of Debussy and Ravel. A famous example is *Prélude à l'Après-midi d'un Faune* by Debussy evoking the imagery of Mallarmé's symbolist poem.

impromptu
A short composition of improvisatory nature usually for piano. Schubert and Chopin wrote in this style.

improvisation or **extemporisation**
   The art of spontaneous composition of music in performance.
   This may take the form of ornamentaion, variation of a song or
   theme, or completely new material. Improvisation is greatly
   used in jazz.

incidental music
   Properly, music to be performed during the action of a play.
   However, the term also includes **overtures** and **interludes**.

inciso (It.)
   Incisive.

indeterminacy
   A modernistic principal since 1945 of leaving elements of
   performance to pure chance (see **aleatoric music**) or letting
   performers decide when to play certain passages. Berio, Cage
   and Stockhausen used this concept in their compositions.

infinite canon
   A never-ending **canon** popularly known as a **round** e.g. *Three
   Blind Mice*.

inglese (It.)
   English.

in modo di (It.)
   In the style or manner of.

innig (Ger.)
   Intimate, heartfelt.

in nomine (Lat., 'in the name of the Lord')
   Title used by 16th and 17th century English composers, e.g.
   Purcell, for polyphonic instrumental compositions based on a
   section of the *benedictus* of Taverner's mass *Gloria Tibi Trinitas*.

instrumentation
   Composing music for particular instruments. This term is used
   with reference to the composer's skill and knowledge of selecting
   instruments which sound well or are unusual, etc.

interlude
(1) Music inserted between other pieces of music, e.g. organ passages between hymn verses. (2) Music inserted between acts of plays or other non-musical events.

intermède (Fr.)
Same as **intermezzo**.

intermezzo (It., 'something in the middle')
(1) An instrumental piece in opera, i.e. performed while the stage is empty. (2) A short concert piece. Brahms wrote in this style. (3) A short comic opera (meaning now obsolete).

interrupted cadence
See **cadence**.

invention
A title used by J.S. Bach for contrapuntal two-part compositions for clavier. Bach called three-part compositions *sinfonie* but they are now also referred to as inventions.

inversion
The turning upside-down of a chord or single melody (by applying intervals in opposite directions) or two melodies in counterpoint by the upper melody becoming the lower and vice-versa. This last method is called *invertible counterpoint*.

ionian mode
The mode which, on the white keys of the piano, is represented from C to C.

isorhythmic (Gk., 'equal-rhythmed')
A device used in **motets** around 1300–1450 in which the rhythmic pattern is repeated according to a strict scheme. This usually occurs in the tenor line in which the rhythm is repeated several times in diminishing note values.

istesso tempo (It.)
At the same tempo.

Italian overture
An orchestral work revealing a literary or pictorial element in

three movements, quick-slow-quick, from which the symphony evolved. The French overture has slow-quick-slow movements.

Italian sixth

A type of augmented sixth chord, e.g. A flat, C and F sharp distinguished by having a major triad and no other note between the notes forming the sixth.

J

jodel
    See **yodel**

jota
    A moderately fast Spanish dance in 3/4 time accompanied by castanets.

K

k

Abbreviation of *köchel* in cataloguing Mozart's works.

kammer (Ger.)

Chamber. *Kammermusik*, chamber music.

KB

Abbreviation of German *Kontrabass*, double-bass.

keen (Ir. *caoine*)

An Irish funeral song accompanied by wailing.

key

This is a musical term to indicate the tonality of a piece based on the **major** or **minor** scales and their relationship between the notes of the scale and chords built around them. There are two types of keys—major or minor—depending upon whether they are based on the notes of the major or minor scale.

key signature

This indicates the precise key of the piece. Sharps or flats are placed at the beginning of a composition after the clef. Any other alteration, e.g. a brief modulation to another key, is indicated by **accidentals**. If there is an extended passage in a new key, however, then a new key signature may appear. The key signature must be represented at the beginning of every new stave in a composition. See table on page 125 for the list of key signatures.

klein (Ger.)

Little.

krakowiak (Pol.)

A quick Polish dance in 2/4 time from the Krakow region.

L

lacrimoso (It.)
Mournful, sad.

lai (Fr.) or **lay**
A type of trouvère song similar to the **sequence** with sections of irregular length and melodic repetition.

lament
Music signifying grief but especially describing bagpipe music played at Scottish clan funerals.

ländler
Slow Austrian dance in waltz time popular in the late 18th and early 19th centuries.

largamente (It.)
Broad and deliberate in style.

larghetto (It., 'a little largo')
Not quite as slow as a **largo**.

largo (It., 'broad')
Slow and broad.

leading note
The seventh degree of the major scale. This is so called because it seems naturally to rise to the tonic a semitone above. In the minor scale this note is used only when ascending, not descending.

lebhaft (Ger.)
Lively.

legato (It.)
Smoothly.

léger (Fr.)
Light. *Légèrement*, lightly.

leggiero, leggieramente (It.)
Light, lightly.

legno (It. 'wood')
(1) Direction in some scores to use the woodblock. (2) Direction to string players to hit the string with the back of the bow. (3) *Bacchetta di legno*, a direction to the drummer to use a wooden-headed drumstick.

leicht (Ger.)
Lightly.

leise (Ger.)
Soft, gentle. *Leiser*, softer.

leitmotif (Ger.)
Leading motif. This is a recurring theme symbolising a character, emotion or object and was first used by H. Von Wolzogen in a discussion of Wagner's *The Ring*.

lento (It.)
Slow.

lesson
This term described a short, keyboard piece or a set of short pieces in the 17th and 18th centuries.

libretto (It., 'booklet')
The text of an **opera** or **oratorio**.

licenza (It.)
Freedom, licence. *Con alcune licenze*, with some freedom in style.

lied (Ger., plural *lieder*)
Song. This term is particularly applied to the German romantic songs of Schubert, Schumann and Brahms. A characteristic is the importance paid to the piano part and the mood of the words.

ligature

(1) In vocal music this is a slur-mark indicating that a group of notes is to be sung to the same syllable. (2) In instrumental music this is a slur indicating notes which are to be phrased together.

loco (It., 'place')

An indication to a performer that music is to be played at the pitch written. This direction may (*a*) cancel previous indications to play at a different pitch or (*b*) indicate a passage to be played in the normal position as opposed to any other in string music.

locrian mode

A mode represented on the white keys of the piano from B to B.

lontano (It.)

Distant.

loud pedal

A vague and misleading term for the sustaining pedal on the piano.

lungo, lunga (It.)

Long.

lusingando, lusinghiero (It.)

Alluringly.

lustig (Ger.)

Cheerful, jolly.

lydian mode

(1) In Ancient Greek music this could be represented on the white keys of the piano from C to C. (2) From the middle ages, the lydian mode can be represented on the white keys of the piano from F to F.

lyric

(1) Words of a song. (2) A fairly short but expressive piece, e.g. *Lyric Piece* by Grieg. (3) Describes vocal performance with the lyre. (4) A lyric drama is an occasional synonym for **opera**.

M

ma (It.)

But.

ma

Abbreviation of the major scale.

madrigal

A secular, polyphonic, unaccompanied vocal composition set to poems for several parts, mainly cultivated in the 16th and 17th centuries. Italian writers of this time included Gabrieli and Palestrina (16th century). Monteverdi and Marenzio wrote in the later highly stylised manner of the 17th century. English writers included Morley and Weelkes.

maestoso (It.)

Majestic, dignified.

maestro (It., 'master')

This title was given to well-known conductors and composers in Italy. It is now used (sometimes rather amusingly) elsewhere.

maggiore (It.)

Major.

maj

Abbreviation of the major scale.

major, minor

These are the two main scales of the western tonal system. The major key is based on the major scale and the minor key is based on the minor scale. The minor scale breaks into three forms: (1) the *harmonic* minor, (2) the *melodic* minor and (3) the *natural* minor. These terms also refer to chords and intervals being built out of the major or minor scale. See table on page 125 for lists of keys.

mal (Ger.)
Time.

malagueña (Sp.)
An Andalusian dance, originating in Málaga, marked by singing. This term also describes an instrumental piece of similar nature.

malinconia (It.)
Melancholy.

marcato (It.)
Marked, emphatic.

march
A marching piece either slow (4/4 time) or quick (2/4 or 6/8 time).

marche (Fr.)
March.

marcia (It.)
March. *Alla marcia*, in a march-like style.

marziale (It.)
Martial.

masque
Aristocratic, elaborate English stage entertainment chiefly cultivated in the 17th century and involving poetry, dancing, scenery, costumes, instrumental and vocal music. The masque was related to **opera** and **ballet**.

mass
This is the main service of the Roman Catholic Church taken in any one of three forms: (1) high mass (*missa solemnis*) which is sung in plainsong; (2) sung mass (*missa cantata*) which is similar to (1) but without a deacon or subdeacon and (3) low mass (*missa privata* or *missa lecta*) which is spoken. However, musicians'

understanding of the mass is the invariable congregational *ordinary of the mass* from the high mass. Composers include Bach, Mozart and Haydn.

mattinata (It.)
Morning song.

mazurka
A Polish folk dance in moderate to fast 3/4 or 3/8 time. Adapted and stylised by Chopin.

MD
Instruction to play with the right hand in piano playing. Abbreviations of *main droite* (Fr.) and *mano destra* (It.).

mediant
A name for the third degree of the scale, e.g. E is in the mediant in C major. The mediant is so-called because it stands between the tonic and dominant.

melisma (Gk., 'song'; plural *melismata*)
Describes a group of notes sung to the same syllable. However, the term is also applied to any florid vocal passage of improvisatory or **cadenza**-like nature.

melodic minor
One of the three types of minor scale.

mélodie (Fr.)
(1) Melody. (2) Song.

melodrama
In musical contexts, this term refers to the dramatic use of the spoken word against a musical background. This style may be used throughout an entire work or just as part of a work.

meno (It.)
Less. *Meno mosso*, slower.

menuet (Fr.), **menuett** (Ger.)
Same as **minuet**.

menuetto
Term used by German composers who believed it to be Italian for minuet. The Italian for minuet is *minuetto*.

messa di voce (It.)
The steady increasing and decreasing of volume on one long held note in singing.

messe (Fr. and Ger.)
Same as **mass**.

mesto (It.)
Sad.

metà (It.)
Half.

metamorphosis of themes
Liszt's term for **leitmotif**, the recurring and development of themes symbolising a character, emotion, object, idea, etc.

metre
This is indicated by a time signature dividing up the music into regularly occurring accents, e.g. 3/4 time means that the basic note values are crotchets and that every third crotchet is accented.

mezzo (It., 'half')
Mezzo-soprano, female voice midway between a soprano and contralto range. *Mezza voce*, with a moderate tone. *Mezzo forte*, midway between loud and soft and abbreviated *mf*.

MG
Instruction to play with the left hand in piano playing. Abbreviation of *main gauche* (Fr.).

mi
Abbreviation of the minor scale.

microtone
An interval smaller than a semitone, evident in some modern compositions.

min
> Abbreviation of the minor scale.

minacciando (It.)
> Threatening.

minim
> Equivalent to two crotchets or half a semibreve. The American term is *half-note*. See table on page 123.

minor
> Opposite of major. Applied to scales, keys, chords and intervals. See entry on **major**.

minuet (Eng.), **minuetto** (It.)
> A moderately fast French dance of rustic origin in 3/4 time but rising to court and becoming fashionable in the 18th century. The minuet is the standard third movement in the classical sonata, symphony, string quartet, etc., developing later into the **scherzo** with Beethoven. Form is A A B A.

mirror
> This term is sometimes attached to a fugue or canon to describe two or more parts appearing simultaneously, with one the correct way up and the other upside down, as if a mirror had been placed between them.

missa (Lat.)
> Mass.

missa brevis (Lat.)
> (1) A short concise musical setting of the mass. (2) A setting of the *Kyrie* and *Gloria* only.

Missa solemnis
> High Mass.

misura (It.)
> A measure. *Senza misura*, not in strict time.

mit (Ger.)
> With.

mixed chorus, mixed voices

A body of singers including both adult male and female voices.

mixolydian mode

A **mode** represented on the white notes of the piano from G to G.

moderato (It.)

At a moderate pace. This term is used in other tempos, e.g. *allegro moderato*, implying a moderately fast pace.

modes

Sets of eight-note scales inherited from ancient Greece via the Middle Ages in which they were most prevalent, although they still survive today in **plainsong** and folk music. At the end of the 17th century the modes had been reduced to two scales, major and minor, which we know today. Here are the modes which may be represented by scales of white notes on the piano with the names derived from the Greek system. The 'final' of a mode is the note of a cadence, or resting point, in a melody, and the 'dominant' is a reciting note.

I	Dorian, D-D, dominant A, final D
II	Hypodorian, AA, dominant F, final D
III	Phrygian, E-E, dominant C, final E
IV	Hypophrygian, B-B, dominant A, final E
V	Lydian, F-F, dominant C, final F
VI	Hypolydian, C-C, dominant A, final F
VII	Mixolydian, G-G, dominant D, final G
VIII	Hypomixolydian, D-D, dominant C, final G

The following were added in the 16th century by Glareanus:

IX	Aeolian, A-A, dominant E, final A
X	Hypoaeolian, E-E, dominant C, final A
XI	Ionian, C-C, dominant G, final C
XII	Hypoionian, G-G, dominant E, final C.

modo (It.)

Manner. *In modo di*, in the manner of.

modulate

The shift from one key to another in composition.

modulator
An old-fashioned diagram used for the teaching of **sol-fa**. Much frowned upon by more progressive music teachers.

molto (It.)
Much, very.

monodrama
A dramatic stage work for only one character, e.g. Schönberg's *Erwartung*.

monody (Gk., 'single song')
A term used to describe a solo song with accompaniment (or **continuo**) in contrast to the polyphonic style in which all parts are of equal importance.

monophony (Gk., 'single sound')
This term describes music with a single melody line without support of accompaniment.

monothematic
Music with only one theme.

morbido (It.)
Gentle, delicate.

mordent
An **ornament** which has two forms: (1) upper mordent (or inverted mordent); (2) lower mordent or simply, mordent.

upper mordent   *lower mordent*

morendo (It.)
Dying away (of force and sometimes, speed).

mosso (It.)
Animated, moving.

motet

(1) In modern use this is a religious choral composition in Latin of the Roman Catholic service corresponding to the **anthem** in the Anglican service. (2) In medieval times, this was a vocal composition based on a given set of words and melody, which sometimes came from a secular song.

motif (Fr.)

(1) A term sometimes used in English for **leitmotif**. (2) Same as **motiv** or **motive**.

motion

A term describing the course of a melody or melodies. *Conjunct motion* is movement by step. *Disjunct motion* is movement by leap. *Similar motion* describes two melodies moving in the same direction and *contrary motion* describes two melodies moving in opposite directions. *Parallel motion* describes parts moving the same way and also keeping the same interval between them.

motiv (Ger.), **motive** (Eng.)

(1) A short but recognisable melodic or rhythmic figure. (2) In analysis, this term describes the smallest subdivision of, e.g. a theme.

moto (It.)

Movement. *Con moto*, with movement.

motto theme

A term for music which recurs and develops in the form of a quotation.

mouth music

English term for Gael. *port a beul* which describes wordless but articulated singing accompanying Scottish Highland dancing when there are no instruments available.

movement

A self-contained section of a large composition having its own time signature and title.

movimento (It.)

Motion. *Doppio movimento*, at double the preceding speed.

MS (It. 'mano sinistra')

Left hand. Instruction to play with left hand in piano playing.

M Sop

Abbreviation of **mezzo soprano**.

musical play

A type of American-influenced light stage entertainment which succeeded the musical comedy in the mid-20th century. Now known simply as a *musical*. An example is *Cats* with music by Andrew Lloyd Webber.

musical switch

A medley of popular tunes.

music drama

A Wagnerian term for **opera**, which he felt to be inadequate. This term describes Wagner's new concept of the **leitmotif** and the fusing of scenery, costume, libretti, music and drama into a new art.

music theatre

A term describing (from the 1960s) dramatic works simpler than opera and suitable for the concert-platform.

musique concrète (Fr., 'concrete music')

Music in which natural sounds (instrumental, vocal or other) were recorded on tape and then distorted, combined, etc. This term was coined by Peter Schaeffer in 1948 but it has largely been superseded by electronic music.

muta (It.)

Change. Direction to the timpani player to change tuning or to the wind player to change instrument.

N

nach (Ger.)
To, after.

nachschlag (Ger.)
Ornament in German music in the 17th and 18th centuries.

nachtanz (Ger., 'after dance')
A quick dance used to follow a slow one.

nachtmusik (Ger.)
Serenade or 'night music'. A title used in Mozart's *Eine Kleine Nachtmusik*.

nationalism, nationalist
Music with national characteristics, e.g. use of folk music. The term is particularly applied to 19th-century composers, e.g. Smetena and Grieg. Bartók and Kodály were also famous as nationalist composers.

natural
(1) The cancelling of a flat or sharp of a note or key indicated by a sign beside the note. (2) A trumpet or horn, etc. not having any valves or keys.

naturale
Instruction to a singer or instrumentalist to perform in the normal way, e.g. singing tenor instead of falsetto or playing without mutes.

neapolitan sixth
A chord on the fourth degree of the scale with a minor third and sixth, e.g. in C major it includes the notes F, A flat and D flat.

neo (Gk., 'new')

A prefix indicating a new interest in older styles, e.g. neo-romantic refers to composers in the 20th century writing in the romantic style.

neo-classical

Describes a trend, especially in the 1920s, characterised by its use of the **concerto grosso** technique, contrapuntal writing and avoidance of emotion. Neo-classical composers included Stravinsky and Hindemith.

new music

(1) In the early 17th century this described the new expressive music. (2) Between 1850 and 1900 it described the new music of Wagner and Liszt as opposed to the more traditional music of Brahms.

niente (It.)

Nothing. *A niente*, to nothing. Used after a diminuendo symbol to indicate the sound dying away entirely.

nobile, nobilmente (It.)

Noble, nobly.

nocturne

A night piece with two main meanings: (1) In the 18th century this was a composition close to a **serenade** for several instruments and movements. (2) In the romantic period it was a short lyrical piece in one movement for piano, e.g. by Chopin.

noël (Fr., 'Christmas')

A Christmas carol.

non (Fr. and It.)

Not.

non-harmonic note

A note which is not part of the chord with which it sounds. This could mean a passing note or an **appoggiatura**.

nota cambiata (It., 'changed note')

A contrapuntal device whereby a dissonant note is used when one expects a consonant one.

notation

Written music, by ordinary staff notation symbols or graphic representation or simply by letter-names, e.g. the tonic sol-fa.

note cluster

The performance of a group of adjacent notes simultaneously on the piano, e.g. with the forearm or a piece of wood. Pioneered by Cowell in 1912 and used by Ives. The American term is *tone cluster*.

note row

This occurs in 20th-century **serial music**, also called *dodecaphonic* music or twelve-note music. It is the order in which the composer chooses to arrange the twelve notes, which serves as the foundation of the composition.

novelette (Eng.) or novellette (Ger.)

A short, instrumental, romantic piece. The term was first used by Schumann for a piano work in 1848.

O

obbligato (It., 'obligatory')

An obbligato part is one which has an important and unusual special role and cannot be dispensed with, as opposed to an optional part. However, in some 19th-century music, the term obbligato was applied to an additional optional part.

oblique motion

Describes the movement of parts or melodies when one remains on the same note and the other moves in some direction.

octave

The interval of eight steps, e.g. C to C on the white notes of the piano.

octet

A composition for eight voices or instruments, or simply eight people.

ode

The setting of a poem entitled 'ode' to music.

ohne (Ger.)

Without.

op

Abbreviation of Latin *opus*, work.

opera

A drama in which all or most characters sing and in which music has an important element. Early composers of opera include

Monteverdi and Purcell. Other composers are Mozart, Beethoven, Rossini, Donizetti, Verdi, Wagner (who preferred the term **music drama**), Puccini, and in the 20th century, Berg and Britten.

opéra bouffe (Fr.)
A light, often satirical opera or operetta, e.g. by Offenbach.

opera buffa (It.)
A comic opera especially in the 18th century, e.g. by Pergolesi.

opéra comique (Fr.)
This term describes comic opera but has two special meanings. (1) A type of French comic opera with spoken dialogue, lighter than current serious operas in the 18th century. (2) An opera, comic or otherwise, with spoken dialogue, e.g. Bizet's *Carmen* in the 19th century.

opera seria (It.)
Serious opera and opposite of **opera buffa**. This term is especially applied to the flourishing 18th-century style as used by Rossini. Characterised by the use of castrato singers, heroic or mythological plots, Italian libretti and formality in the music and action.

opera-ballet
A stage work giving more or less equal importance to opera and ballet, e.g. the works of Lully and Rameau in France in the 17th and 18th centuries.

opera oratorio
A stage work involving elements of both **opera** and **oratorio**, e.g. Stravinsky's *Oedipus Rex*.

operetta (It., 'little opera')
A term applied in the 19th century to lighter styles of opera involving dialogue. Composers included Offenbach, Johann Strauss and Sullivan. This style is sometimes referred to as *light opera*.

opérette (Fr.)
Operetta.

oratorio
> A musical composition (originating around 1600) consisting of an extended setting of a religious or epic text for chorus, soloists and orchestra for performance in a church or concert hall, although originally oratorios involved scenery, costumes and action. An example is Handel's *Messiah* of 1742.

orchestra
> A large body of instrumentalists which has developed historically. The first orchestras were variable, but by the baroque period they consisted of strings, oboes and bassoons with other solo instruments. Standardisation took place in the classical period when the orchestra was divided into four sections: strings, woodwind (two flutes, two oboes, two bassoons and clarinets), brass (two horns and two trumpets) and percussion consisting of two kettledrums. The orchestra was greatly expanded in the 19th century to include the harp and other percussion. Some 20th-century composers reacted against the large orchestra and used smaller groupings.

orchestration
> (1) The art of writing for an orchestra, band, etc., involving great knowledge of tone-colours, range of instruments, technical capacities and combinations of instruments, etc. (2) The scoring of a work, originally intended for another medium, for an orchestra.

organum
> A medieval type of part-writing based on plainsong and harmonised by either one, two or three parallel parts.

ornaments
> Also called *graces* or *embellishments*, these are notes considered to be an extra embellishment of a melody which are either added spontaneously by the performer or indicated by the composer on the score by signs or notation. In the 17th and 18th centuries, ornaments were mostly indicated by signs and they included the **trill, mordent, turn, arpeggio** and **appoggiatura**. Composers wrote out ornaments in full in later periods.

ossia (It.)
> Or. Indicates an alternative passage (usually a simpler version) in a composition.

71

ostinato (It., 'obstinate')

A persistently repeated musical figure or rhythm. A *basso ostinato* or ground bass has this feature in the bass part.

ôtez (Fr.)

Take off. *Ôtez les sourdines*, take off the mutes.

ottava (It.)

Octave. Often written 8ve. *All'ottava*, at the octave and *ottava bassa*, an octave lower.

overtone

Any notes of the **harmonic series** are given this name except for the first **fundamental**.

overture

(1) An orchestral piece preceding an opera, oratorio or play. (2) Since Mendelssohn's *Hebrides* of 1832, the overture also describes a one-movement orchestral piece composed for the concert hall with a non-musical subject. This is also called the *concert overture*. (3) In the 17th and 18th centuries the French overture (preceding an opera, etc.) was in three movements, slow-quick-slow, and the Italian overture (a precursor of the symphony) also in three movements was quick-slow-quick.

P

p

Abbreviaion for **piano** (It.), soft. Varying degrees of softness are abbreviated as *pp.*, *ppp*. etc.

pantomime

(1) Traditionally a play in dumb-show or mime. (2) Nowadays it is a Christmas stage entertainment based on a fairy-story or other traditional source with dialogue, popular songs, costumes and actions e.g. *Snow White, Alladin* etc.

pantonality

Schönberg preferred this term to atonality i.e. music not written in any definite key.

parallel motion

The movement of two or more parts in the same direction while also keeping the same interval between them.

parody mass (Lat. *missa parodia*)

A polyphonic mass, e.g. by Palestrina, flourishing in the 16th century based on existing material of a **motet** or **chanson**. This term has only been used since the 19th century, however.

part

The music of a particular voice or instrument in an ensemble.

parte (It.)

Voice-part.

partials

The tones of the **harmonic series**, the lowest being the *first partial* and the others the *upper partials* or *overtones*.

partita (It.)

A suite. This term was much used in the 18th century. In the 17th century, however, a partita was a **variation**.

part-song

Generally a strophic song for several male, female or mixed voices in which there are many singers to a part, with the top part usually having the principal part. Composers include Elgar, Parry and Stanford.

part-writing

The composing of polyphonic music and the writing of equally good melodic parts.

pas (Fr.)

Step. A *pas d'action* is a ballet scene of dramatic nature and a *pas de deux* is a dance for two.

pasodoble (Sp., 'double step') or **paso doble**

A modern and quick Spanish dance in 2/4 time.

passacaglia

Originally a slow and stately dance appearing in keyboard music of the 17th century. Later the passacaglia was a piece with a theme continually repeated, but not necessarily in the bass, like the **chaconne**.

passage

A section of a composition, usually with no structural importance.

passing note

A note, which may be accented or unaccented, forming a discord with the chord with which it is heard, but is melodically placed between two consonant notes.

passion music

This is the Passion of Christ, as accounted by Matthew, Mark, Luke and John, set to music and properly performed during Holy Week.

pasticcio (It., 'pie')

An operatic work with the material drawn from the works of various composers, especially popular in the 18th century.

pastiche (Fr.)

A piece composed deliberately in the style of another well-known composer. See also **pasticcio** above.

pastoral

(1) Alternative name for the **madrigal**. (2) Any piece representing country life.

pastorale (It.)

(1) An instrumental movement with long bass notes giving a drone-like effect in 6/8 or 12/8 time. (2) Obsolete term for a stage entertainment based on a legendary or rustic subject, e.g. Handel's *Acis and Galatea*.

patter song

Popular in opera, this is a comic song in which words, sung as fast as possible, are often tongue-twisters. Often found in the works of Gilbert and Sullivan.

pausa (It.)

A rest (not a pause).

pause

A wait of indefinite length on a note or rest.

pavan (Eng.) or **pavane** (Fr.)

A slow, stately dance usually in duple time dating from the 16th century. It was normally followed by the quicker **galliard** after about 1550, often employing the same theme.

ped

(1) In piano music, this is an indication for the sustaining pedal to be depressed.

(2) In organ music, it is an indication that the music is to be played on the pedal keyboard.

pedal

The *fundamental* or lowest note of the **harmonic series** especially applied to the playing of brass instruments.

pedal point

A note, usually in the bass, which is held below changing harmonies above, with which it may be discordant.

pentatonic

A five-note scale, the commonest being without minor seconds, for example CDEGA(C).

per (It.)

By, through, for, e.g. *per archi*, for strings.

perdendosi (It., 'losing itself')

Gradually dying away.

perfect cadence

A cadence with the chord progression consisting of the dominant (chord V) to the tonic (chord I) which has a 'complete' sound.

perfect intervals

These are the intervals of the octave, fourth and fifth.

perfect pitch

A sense of pitch which enables a person to identify a note simply by hearing it.

perfect time

In medieval music, this was triple time.

perpetual canon

Popularly known as a round, this is a never-ending **canon** which is also known as an *infinite canon*.

perpetuum mobile (Lat., 'perpetually in motion')

A fast piece of music in which a rapid repetitive note-pattern is played throughout.

pesante (It.)

Heavy, ponderous.

petit (Fr.)
Little.

petto (It., 'chest')
In musical contexts used as in *voci di petto*, chest voice.

phantasie (Ger.)
Fantasy.

phrase
A group of notes forming a unit of a melody. To phrase a melody is to observe and mark the divisions of a melody into units or phrases.

phrygian cadence
A cadence which ends on the dominant of the relative minor e.g. in C major, the final chord would be E, G sharp, B.

phrygian mode
The mode which, on the white keys of the piano, is represented by E to E.

piacere a (It.)
At pleasure, i.e. not at any strict speed.

piacevole (It.)
Pleasantly.

piangendo (It.)
Plaintively.

pianissimo (It.)
Very soft, with abbreviation *pp*.

piano (It.)
(1) Soft, abbreviation *p*. (2) Standard abbreviation in French and English for pianoforte.

pibroch (Gael. *piobaireachd*)
Scottish Highland bagpipe music consisting of variations on a theme (*urlar*) and many **grace-notes**.

picardy third or **tierce de picardie** (Fr.)
The surprising sound of a major third at the end of a piece otherwise in a minor key thus converting the expected minor chord to a major one. This was a common device up to the mid-18th century.

più (It.)
More. *Più lento*, slower.

piuttosto (It.)
Somewhat, rather.

pizz
Abbreviation of **pizzicato**.

pizzicato (It.)
Indication to pluck notes on a bowed string instrument. Abbreviation *pizz*.

plagal cadence
A closing cadence consisting of a progression of the subdominant (chord IV) to the tonic (Chord I) sounding like 'Amen'.

plainchant or **plainsong** (from Lat. *cantus planus*)
Medieval church music usually describing the gregorian chant which still survives today in the Roman Catholic church. It consists of a single, unaccompanied vocal line in free rhythm like speech with no regular bar lengths.

pneuma (Gk., 'breath')
A type of florid passage in plainsong sung to a single vowel.

pochettino, pochetto (It.)
Very slightly, very little. Diminutive of **poco**.

pochissimo (It.)
Very slightly. Superlative of **poco**.

poco (It.)
Slightly, little, rather. *Poco crescendo*, getting slightly louder and *poco a poco*, little by little.

poi (It.)
Then. In the phrase *scherzo da capo, e poi la coda* it means repeat the scherzo and then go on to the coda.

pointe d'archet (Fr.)
Point of the bow.

pointillism
Term taken from painting (referring to pictures using separate dots of colour) and applied to the music of some 20th-century composers e.g. Webern. This described music of a spare and pointed style emplying use of **pizzicato**.

polacca (It.)
See **polonaise**.

polka
A moderately fast dance in 2/4 time for couples, originating in Bohemia in the 19th century and becoming popular in Europe and the US.

polo
A Spanish dance in fast, syncopated 3/4 time with song.

polonaise
A stately Polish dance in moderately fast 3/4 time dating from at least the 16th century. Composers include Bach, but the most famous examples are the 13 written by Chopin.

polychoral
Term describes the use of several choirs performing both separately and jointly in a composition.

polymetry or **polymetrical**
The combining of different metres simultaneously, e.g. 2/4 against 3/4 or 6/8.

polyphony
A style of music in two or more parts in which (as opposed to **homophony**) each part is independent and of equal importance. Therefore, polyphonic music implies the use of counterpoint, and some of the most important forms are the **motet, canon** and **fugue**. Composers include Palestrina, Byrd and Bach.

polyrhythm

The systematic use of quite different rhythms sounding simultaneously. Polyrhythmic devices are especially used in the 20th century.

polytonality

The use of two or more keys performed simultaneously and employed by Stravinsky, Holst and Milhaud. When only two keys are used, this is referred to as *bitonality*.

pomposo (It.)

In a pompous manner.

port a beul (Gael.)

Same as **mouth music**.

portamento (It.)

Carrying sound. On bowed string instruments or in singing, the effect is obtained by gliding from one note to another higher or lower one, without a break in the sound.

position

(1) In string playing, the term indicates where on the fingerboard the left hand should be in order to play a passage. (2) In trombone playing, the term indicates how far the slide should be pushed out. (3) In harmony, the term describes the layout of a chord. Here are the common positions of the chord with C major as an example, using the notes C E and G. In *root position*, the chord of C is played with C (the root of the chord) at the bottom. In *first inversion*, the chord is played with E at the bottom. In *second inversion* the chord is played with G at the bottom. Therefore, the note at the bottom of the chord determines these positions.

postlude

A final piece of a composition.

poussé (Fr.)

Up bow as opposed to *tiré*, down bow.

pp

Abbreviation for **pianissimo**, very soft.

precipitato, precipitoso (It.)
Impetuously.

preciso (It.)
Precise.

preclassical
Term describing music before Haydn and Mozart and also (more vaguely) describing music before Bach.

prelude
An introductory piece or movement before a fugue, an act of an opera etc. Chopin and other later composers wrote preludes as short, independent piano pieces in one movement.

preparation
A harmonic device in which the effect of a discord is softened by first employing the note which actually causes that chord to be discordant, in the previous note with which it is consonant.

prepared piano
A 20th-century term, coined by John Cage, describing a piano which has been prepared by the insertion of objects between the piano strings for performance, e.g. a piece of cardboard.

pressez (Fr.)
Increase speed.

prestissimo (It.)
Very fast. Superlative of **presto**.

presto (It.)
Fast. In Mozart's music this means as fast as possible.

prima, primo (It.)
First.

prima donna (It., 'first lady')
A female singer with the most important part in an opera.

prima volta (It.)
First time.

primo (It.)

First. (1) Upper part of a piano duet, the lower part being termed *secondo*. (2) The first of two or more performers e.g. *violino primo* means first violin. (3) *Tempo primo* indicates that the original speed is to be resumed.

primo vomo (It.)

The chief castrato or tenor role, used in the 18th century.

principal

(1) The first player of an orchestral section, e.g. the 'principal horn'. (2) In opera, the principal is the singer who performs the main parts, but not the chief ones.

programme music

Music which interprets or describes a story, painting, poem, landscape or emotional experience. Opposite of **absolute music**.

progression

The movement from one note or chord to another in music.

progressive tonality

The systematic plan of beginning in one key and ending in another in a movement, used e.g. by Nielsen and Mahler.

punta d'arco (It.)

Point of the bow.

Q

quadrille
A French square dance popular in the 19th century. It was in five sections alternating between 6/8 and 2/4 time and performed by two or four couples.

quadruple counterpoint
Counterpoint in which four melodies can exchange position.

quadruple fugue
A **fugue** with four different subjects.

quadruple stop
A chord of four notes played on a bowed string instrument.

quadruplet
A group of four notes to be played in the time of 3.

quadruple time
Same as **common time** consisting of four crotchets to the bar, written 4/4 or C.

quarter note
American term for crotchet. See table on page 123.

quarter tone
Half a semitone, and the smallest interval traditionally used in western music in the 20th century, e.g. by Bloch, Hába, Boulez and Stockhausen.

quartet
A composition for four performers.

quasi

quasi (It.)
As if, almost.

quaver
The note equivalent to half a crotchet or two semiquavers. American term is 'eighth note'. See table on page 123.

quest opera
An opera in which the principal character undergoes a test or a difficult journey, or experiences hardships before reaching his goal e.g. Mozart's *The Magic Flute*.

quickstep
A modern ballroom dance with quick steps.

quintet
A composition for five performers.

quintuplet
A group of five notes to be performed in the time of 4.

quintuple time
Time with five beats, usually crotchets, to the bar, e.g. 5/4 time. Not common before the 20th century.

quodlibet (Lat., 'what you will')
A piece containing several popular tunes. The composition may be improvised or notated and was especially practised by German composers (e.g. Bach) in the 17th and 18th centuries.

R

R

Abbreviation of (1) Ray in the tonic sol-fa. (2) Respond.

rabbia (It.)

Rage.

raddoppiamento (It.)

Doubling. Usually indicates doubling of the bass at an octave below.

rall

Abbreviation of **rallentando**.

rallentando (It.)

Getting slower.

rant

Describes a wide range of 17th-century English dances.

rasch (Ger.)

Quick.

ratsche (Ger.)

Rattle.

real answer

A responding musical phrase, e.g. in a **fugue**, which exactly reproduces the subject or entry of a theme at the fifth.

realisation

The completion of 17th- and 18th-century harmony by adding a keyboard accompaniment indicated by **figured bass**.

recapitulation
Particularly used in **sonata form**, this term describes a section of a composition which repeats or approximates themes originally presented in a previous section, which have since been developed.

recit
Abbreviation of **recitative**.

récit (Fr.)
(1) **Recitative**. (2) Swell organ.

recital
A performance by one or two performers.

recitative
Generally, this is a style of singing used in opera and oratorio for dialogue and some narrative which is more closely related to dramatic speech in pitch and rhythm than to song. Two main types exist: (1) *recitative accompagnato* or *stromentato* which is expressive and accompanied by the orchestra and (2) *recitative secco* which has only an occasional broken chord from the harpsichord or 'cellos (sometimes with the bass line reinforced by the double-bass) and this was the accepted style in 18th- and 19th-century operas.

recueilli (Fr.)
Meditative, collected.

redundant entry
In a **fugue**, this term describes an extra voice in the initial entries or exposition.

reel
A fast dance for two or more couples in 2/4 or 4/4 time, found mainly in Scotland, Ireland, Scandinavia and North America.

refrain
A recurring section of a song (both words and music) at the end of each stanza.

register
> (1) The division of compass of a singer's voice, e.g. *chest register* and *head register*. Also applied to the compass of an instrument, e.g. the *chalumeau* register of the clarinet. (2) A set of organ pipes controlled by one particular stop.

réjouissance (Fr., 'enjoyment')
> This title is sometimes found in spirited movements in suites of the **baroque** period.

related
> Describes the harmonic relationships of keys, e.g. G major is closely related to D major (its dominant) since there is only the difference of one sharp. See also **relative**.

relative
> This term refers to each key signature being shared by two keys, e.g. A minor is the 'relative' minor of C major since they both have no sharps or flats in the key signature. D major is the relative major of B minor since both keys have two sharps in the key signature.

repeat
> A restatement of a section of a composition usually indicated by repeat marks which consist of a pair of dots and a double bar. When the performer reaches these repeat marks, he then plays from the previous pair of dots, or if there are none, from the beginning.

répétiteur (Fr.)
> The coach, usually in an opera house, who teaches singers their parts. The répétiteur may also give them cues during the performance.

répétition (Fr.)
> Rehearsal. *Répétition Générale* is the dress rehearsal, often given before a full, but invited audience, in continental opera houses.

replica (It.)
> Repeat.

reprise (Fr.)
(1) Repeat. (2) The recapitulation in **sonata form**. (3) The return to the first section after contrasting music in the second section in **binary form**.

resolution
In harmony this is the progression from a discord to a concord.

respond, responsory
A plainsong chant sung by a chorus alternating with solo verse(s).

rest
A silence in a performer's part indicated by symbols corresponding to certain beats. See table on page 123.

retardation
In harmony this is a **suspension** which resolves upwards not downwards.

retenu (Fr.)
Held back.

retrograde motion
A theme which is played backwards. This device was prominent in the Middle Ages in fugues and in 20th-century **serial music**. *Retrograde inversion* describes a theme played backwards and upside-down.

rezitativ (Ger.)
Recitative.

rf, rfz
Abbreviations of **rinforzando**.

rh
Abbreviation for right hand.

rhapsody
A title given by 19th- and 20th-century composers to describe works generally in one continuous movement suggestive of heroic, national or other romantic inspiration.

riddle canon
> A **canon** in which the composer leaves the performer to decide where and at what pitch the following voices make their entries.

rigadoon (Eng.), **rigaudon** (Fr.)
> A lively old French dance in 2/4 or 4/4 time.

rinf
> Abbreviation of **rinforzando**.

rinforzando (It.)
> Reinforcing. A sudden strong accent on notes or chords. Similar to **sforzando**. Abbreviations are *rf, rfz, rinf.*

ripieno (It.)
> In the old **concerto grosso**, the ripieno indicates the full body of performers as opposed to the solo group (*concertino*). *Senza ripieni* indicates that the first **desks** only of the accompanying orchestra are to play.

risoluto (It.)
> In a resolute manner.

risvegliato (It.)
> Animated.

rit
> Abbreviation of **ritardando**.

ritardando (It.)
> Becoming slower. Abbreviation is *rit.*

ritenuto (It.)
> Held back (tempo). Sometimes used as an equivalent of **ritardando**.

ritmo (It.)
> Rhythm. *Ritmo di tre battute* indicates that the music is to be performed in three- bar groupings, implying that the music is so fast there is only one beat to the bar.

ritornello (It. 'a little return')
> Many meanings, but the following are the most common. (1) In

89

a concerto, it is a passage for the full orchestra without the soloist. (2) In the 14th-century Italian madrigal, the ritornello is the closing section. (3) In early opera, it was an instrumental piece.

rococo

This term was taken from French culture in the early 18th century, but musically the title for rococo is the **style galant** used by composers throughout Europe until the late 18th century.

roll

A rapid succession of notes on a drum approximating to a continuous sound.

romance (Eng. and Fr.), romanze (Ger.), romanza (It.)

The term has been used widely, but it often implies an intimate and lyrical piece for voice or instrument.

romanesca

Evident in the mid-16th and early 17th century, this was a harmonic bass line used for variations.

romantic music

A 19th-century style expressed by writers, painters and by musicians like Chopin, Liszt, Berlioz, Rossini and Paganini. Characteristics are lyricism, chromatic harmony, an interest in literature, nationalism, programme music, miniature or character pieces and generally emotional aspects governing the traditional, formal musical structures.

rondeau (Fr.)

A type of French medieval song of the 13th to 15th centuries with a choral refrain. This French spelling was used in instrumental works of the baroque period to describe **rondo**.

rondo (It.)

Generally, an instrumental composition in which one section recurs at certain times. By the 18th century, a standard pattern had developed as A B A C A D A, etc. appearing as the last movement of a sonata or concerto. The recurring theme A is called the *rondo theme* and B C D, etc. represent the contrasting sections known as *episodes*. However, A can be varied. The combination of sonata form and rondo resulted in **sonata rondo** which was much used by Mozart and Beethoven.

root

The lowest or fundamental note of a chord, e.g. in the chord C E G, C is the root and the chord is said to be in *root position*. If the notes are arranged E G C, C is still the root, but the chord would be described as being in *first inversion*.

rota (Lat., 'wheel')

Occasionally this term is used for the **round**, e.g. of *Sumer is Icumen In*.

round

A short vocal perpetual canon in which voices enter in turn to sing a melody at the octave or at the same pitch, e.g. *London's Burning*.

rubato (It., 'robbed')

An indication to play notes with a controlled flexibility of time by getting slightly quicker or slower. Much used in 19th-century music.

rumba

A fast, syncopated and suggestive Afro-Cuban dance in 2/4 time, divided into eight beats. Became popular in the ballroom and jazz in the 1930s.

S

saltarello or **salterello** (It.)

A quick Italian dance in 6/8 time similar to the **tarantella** with a characteristic jumping feel to the rhythm. Examples date from the 14th century.

samba

A quick, highly syncopated Brazilian carnival song danced usually in 2/4 time in a circle with a standard call and response between lead singer and chorus. The ballroom version is danced in couples and is more sedate.

sarabande

A slow and stately dance in 3/2 or 3/4 time, usually in binary form and one of the standard elements of the **suite**.

sardana (Sp.)

A Catalonian national dance performed to pipes and drums, often in sections. Similar to the **farandole**.

satz (Ger.)

A setting. (1) A musical setting. (2) A movement in a composition. (3) Style, e.g. *freier satz*, free style. (4) A theme or subject, e.g. *hauptsatz*, first subject.

scale

A progression of single notes in ascending or descending order. A scale may be described as **major, minor, chromatic, diatonic, pentatonic, twelve-note** or a **mode**.

scena (It., 'stage' or 'scene')

(1) A scene in an opera consisting of an extended aria of dramatic nature. (2) A dramatic concert piece for solo voice with accompaniment.

scherzando (It.)
Playfully, light-hearted.

scherzetto or **scherzino** (It.)
A short **scherzo**.

scherzo (It., 'joke')
Generally this is a lively movement, but chiefly developed by Haydn, Mozart and particularly Beethoven from the symphonic minuet. Usually it is in 3/4 time in the form A A B A with the B section being called *trio*.

schlag (Ger.)
Beat.

schleppen (Ger.)
To drag. *Schleppend*, dragging.

schluss (Ger.)
End.

schlüssel (Ger.)
Clef.

schnell (Ger.)
Fast. *Schneller*, quicker.

schottische (Ger. plural, 'Scottish')
A popular 19th-century ballroom dance similar to the **polka**.

schmetternd (Ger., 'blaring')
An indication to horn players to use a harsh brassy tone.

schrittmässig or **schrittweise** (Ger.)
Stepwise, at a walking pace and equivalent of **andante**.

schwach (Ger.)
Weak, soft.

schwindend (Ger.)
Dying away, fading.

schwung (Ger.)
Swing. *Schwungvol*, spirited.

scoop
To slide up to a note in singing instead of hitting it accurately.

score
Notated music of all performers' parts combined in an ordered form in which each part appears vertically above another. A *piano score* is one in which all orchestral or even vocal parts are reduced to a piano part. A *miniature* or *pocket score* reproduces all parts and details of the full score but is of a size more suitable for study.

scorrevole (It.)
Scurrying, rapid.

Scotch snap
A rhythmic figure consisting of a short note on the beat followed by a longer one held until the next beat. Found in Scottish music but also in other folk music.

sec (Fr., 'dry')
An indication that a note or chord is to be played sharply.

secco
This word is associated with **recitative**.

secondary dominant
This describes the dominant of the dominant, e.g. D in the key of C (major or minor) since G is the dominant of C and D is the dominant of G.

segno (It.)
Sign. *Dal segno*, from the sign. This means the performer must repeat the passage from the appropriate sign.

segue (It., 'it follows')
An indication that the performer should go straight on to the next section without a break.

seguidilla (Sp.)
A quick Spanish dance with singing in 3/4 time often with castanets and similar to the **bolero**.

sehr (Ger.)
Very.

semibreve
The note equivalent to two minims. The American term is *whole note*. See table on page 123.

semiquaver
The note equivalent to half a quaver or two demisemiquavers. The American term is *sixteenth note*. See table on page 123.

semitone
The smallest interval commonly used in European music. On the piano this is represented by the interval between any note and the next note which may be higher or lower, e.g. F (white note) and F sharp (black note).

semplice (It.)
Simple, simply.

sempre (It.)
Always. *Sempre più mosso*, always getting faster.

senza (It.)
Without.

septet
(1) A group of seven performers which may consist of instrumentalists or singers. (2) A composition for seven performers which, if for instrumentalists, will have the character of a **sonata** in several movements.

septuplet
A group of seven notes to be played in the time of 4 or 6.

sequence
Generally, this is a phrase repeated at a higher or lower interval. A *real sequence* is one in which the repeated phrase intervals are unaltered. A *tonal sequence* is one in which the repeated phrase is modified to prevent a key change.

serenade

A vague term with two main meanings. (1) A romantic love song, properly performed in the night air accompanied by mandolin or guitar in order to woo a girl. (2) Evening entertainment (especially 18th-century) comprising a set of instrumental movements for chamber orchestra or wind group similar to the **divertimento**. The German equivalent is *nachtmusik*.

serenata (It.)

An English 18th-century term to describe a type of **cantata** approaching operatic form, e.g. Handel's *Acis and Galatea*.

serial music

Also known as *twelve-tone music* (American), *twelve-note music* (British) and *dodecaphonic music*. This is a 20th-century concept mostly developed by Schönberg. A twelve-note theme is fixed upon, with each note being used once. This is known as the *tone row* or *series*. Thereafter it can appear in four main ways: (1) forwards, (2) backwards (*retrograde*), (3) upside down (*inversion*) and (4) upside down and backwards (*retrograde inversion*). The series can appear and begin on any one of the twelve pitches and more than one note of the series can be used simultaneously to form a chord. Serialism mostly forms the basis of a work, however, and other composers include Berg and Webern. Serialism is a feature of **expressionism**.

series

See **serial music** above.

sextuplet or **sextolet**

A group of six notes to be peformed in the time of 4.

sfogato (It., 'evaporated')

Light and airy playing. The term was used by Chopin.

sforzando, sforzato (It.)

With a forced manner (of a note or chord). Abbreviation is *sf*.

shake

Alternative name for **trill**.

shanty

A sailors' work song with solo verses (often of an extemporised nature) and chorus matching certain rhythmical movements, e.g. pulling a rope together.

sharp

A rise in pitch which may be a semitone, or a description of someone singing or playing sharp unintentionally. A *double sharp* indicates a rising of the pitch by two semitones. See table on page 125 for notation.

sight-reading or **sight-singing**

The reading or singing of music at sight, i.e. music which has not been seen before. A traditional element in music examinations.

signature

See **key signature** and **time signature**. A *signature tune* is played by a dance band or orchestra as a means of identification of a television or radio programme, etc.

similar motion

Two melodies moving together in the same direction.

simile (It., 'similar')

Indicates that a phrase, etc. is to be performed in the same manner as the previous one.

simple time

Time in which each beat is divisible by two, e.g. 2/4, 4/4, 3/4 and in which each beat is a crotchet.

sinfonia

Small orchestras currently perform under this name. Originally the title described an instrumental piece in the **baroque** era such as the prelude, overture to an opera, cantata or suite.

sinfonia concertante (It.)

Haydn and Mozart's preferred title to **concerto** for an orchestral work with more than one solo parts.

sinfonie or **symphonie** (Ger.)

Symphony.

sinfonietta (It.)

A shorter, lighter **symphony**. Also sometimes used as a performing name for small orchestras.

singspiel (Ger., 'play with singing')

Generally the singspiel is a comic opera with spoken dialogue in the local dialect instead of **recitative**. An example is Mozart's *The Magic Flute* (1791). In the early 19th century the style combined with German romantic opera and later came to be known simply as 'German musical comedy'.

sinistra (It.)

Left hand.

sitz-probe (Ger.)

An opera term for a 'sitting rehearsal' when all performers sing through the roles whilst sitting down, with the accompaniments played by the orchestra.

six-four chord

The chord containing the sixth and fourth intervals from the bass note. Also known as the *second inversion*, e.g. the 6/4 chord G C E is the second inversion of C E G.

sixteenth note

American term for semiquaver. See table on page 123.

six-three chord

The chord containing the sixth and third intervals from the bass note. Same as *first inversion*, e.g. the 6/3 chord E G C is the first inversion of C E G.

slentando (It.)

Becoming slower.

slide

Device on some brass instruments, used principally on the trombone, for altering the length of the tube, and therefore the notes produced.

slur

A curved line grouping notes together, indicating that they be joined smoothly in performance, i.e. sung in one breath or played with one stroke of the bow, etc.

smorzando (It.)
Dying away.

soave (It.)
Sweetly, tenderly.

soft pedal
The left-foot pedal on a piano lessening the volume.

sol-fa
An English system of notation and sight-reading mainly devised by J.S. Curwen in the 1840s. The notes of the major scale are named in ascending order: doh, ray, me, fah, soh, lah, te, doh. Doh is the tonic, or keynote, but is not at any fixed pitch.

solfeggio (It.), **solfège** (Fr.)
Ear-training by singing exercises to **sol-fa** syllables. More advanced forms are sung to vowels known as *vocalizzi* (It.) or *vocalises* (Fr.).

solo (It., 'alone')
A piece or passage for one performer. A *solo concerto* is a concerto for one main performer with the others merely accompanying.

soltanto (It.)
Solely.

sonata
(1) Before 1750 this described any composition for a solo instrument or for one or more instruments accompanied by **continuo** and not in any strict form. (2) Since 1750 (i.e. the classical period onwards) the sonata became a three- or four-movement work for solo instrument or for solo instrument with piano accompaniment. A similar work for three performers (often two violins and 'cello) is called a *trio sonata*. A violin sonata or 'cello sonata, etc. implies a piano accompaniment. The form of the first movement of the sonata was a feature and it became known as **sonata form**.

sonata da camera or **chamber sonata**

The term was applied to a work, e.g. by Corelli, from the 17th century, written usually for strings and keyboard background in several contrasting movements resembling dances from a **suite** preceded by a **prelude**.

sonata da chiesa (It., 'church sonata')

Similar to **sonata da camera** and in several movements but of a graver nature avoiding dance movements. Mostly trio sonatas, Corelli's examples have four contrasting movements, slow-fast-slow-fast.

sonata form

Also called *first movement form* and *compound binary form*. This structure is most used since 1750 for the first movements and sometimes slow and final movements of a sonata, quartet, symphony or overture. The form is divided into three distinct sections (sometimes after a slow introduction). (1) The *exposition* presents the first main subject in the home key, and a contrasting second subject in another key, which is generally the dominant if in a major key, or relative major if in a minor key. A closing theme is then heard related to the first subject, and brought to an end with a **codetta**. (2) The *development* consists of material already presented but expanded and developed upon. (3) The *recapitulation* presents a varied repetition of the exposition, now influenced by the development section and ending in the tonic key. The codetta now develops into a **coda**.

sonata rondo

A combination of **sonata form** and **rondo form**. In a rondo the five sections are A B A C A. In sonata rondo these become A B A C A B plus coda in which A becomes the first subject, B becomes the second subject and C becomes the development section. This form was much used by Beethoven.

sonatina (It.), **sonatine** (Fr.)

A little **sonata**. Shorter, lighter and generally easier to play than a sonata.

song cycle

A set of songs performed in its entirety and set to words by a single poet. Beethoven wrote the first example in 1816, *An die*

Ferne Geliebte. In the romantic era, however, Schumann and Schubert used traditional German popular song combined with more imaginative accompaniment to illuminate and interpret words in a romantic way. An example is *Die Winterreise* ('Winter Journey') composed in 1828 by Schubert.

song form

A title given to the basic A B A form or *ternary form* as used in an instrumental slow movement. However, this is rather vague and is best avoided since not every song is in this form.

sonore (Fr.), sonoro (It.)

With full tone.

sons bouchés (Fr.)

Stopped notes on the horn.

sons étouffés (Fr.)

Damped sound. Mostly found in harp music indicating that the performer should dampen vibrations immediately after plucking, to produce a 'dry' sound.

sopra (It., 'above')

Usually found in piano music indicating that one hand has to pass over the other.

soprano

Highest female voice with range approximately extending from middle C to two octaves above that. Boy trebles can also achieve this range. The term is also applied to some instruments, e.g. soprano saxophone.

sordino (It.)

Mute. (1) Of a string or wind instrument, *con sordino* or *con sordini* means with mute(s). *Senza sordino* or *senza sordini* means without mutes. (2) In piano playing *senza sordini* indicates that dampers are to be raised and the performer is to use the sustaining, or right-hand pedal. Alternative and more common term is *ped*.

sostenuto (It.)

Sustained, in a smooth manner. The sostenuto pedal on the piano is the middle pedal, only fitted on more expensive instruments. This enables the performer to select notes he wishes to be sustained.

sotto voce (It.)
Whispered, barely audible. This term is applicable to both instrumental and vocal music.

soubrette (Fr., 'cunning')
In opera or operetta, this often describes a soprano singing the role of a shrewd, rather pert servant girl.

soutenu (Fr.)
Sustained and flowing.

speech-song
See **sprechgesang**.

spezzato (It., 'divided')
Cori spezzati, divided choirs. A term used in connection with 16th- and 17th-century Venetian church choruses.

spianato (It.)
Smooth.

spiccato (It.)
Clearly articulated. This term is used in string playing for a light, staccato touch created by playing with the middle of the bow and a loose wrist.

spieltenor (Ger.)
A light tenor voice in opera.

spinto (It.)
Urged on, pushed.

spirito, spiritoso (It.)
Spirit, spirited.

spiritual
A type of religious American Negro folk-song with a call and response pattern.

sprechgesang (Ger.)

Speechsong. Voice delivery midway between song and speech, used mostly by Schönberg although he preferred the terms *sprechstimme* (speaking voice), *sprechmelodie* (speech melody) or *rezitation*. An 'x' on the note stem has become the standard indication on a score for sprechgesang to be used with an approximation of the pitch. An example of a work employing sprechgesang is Schönberg's *Pierrot Lunaire*.

stabreim (Ger.)

Alliteration. This term describes the alliterative verse used by Wagner in his music dramas.

staccato (It., 'detached')

The note is performed shorter than normal. A dash beneath or above the note indicates that the note is to be played as short as possible. A dot means the note is to be short. The superlative is *staccatissimo*.

staff or **stave**

The set of five horizontal lines and spaces on which music is written. Leger lines are used for notes above and below the staff.

stark (Ger.)

Loud, strong.

stentando (It.)

Labouring, holding back on each note.

stile (It.)

Style. *Stile rappresentativo* describes the style of dramatic **recitative** used in early operas and oratorios.

stopping

(1) On stringed instruments, this is the placing of the left-hand fingers on the strings to shorten the vibrating length and to raise the pitch. The terms *double stopping, triple stopping*, etc. refer to two or three notes simultaneously being played this way. (2) In horn playing, this is the insertion of the hand into the bell of the instrument to alter the pitch and tone quality of a note.

strascinando (It.)
Dragging.

strathspey
A Scottish dance related to the reel with a slower tempo and characteristic rhythms with four beats to the bar.

strepitoso (It.)
Noisy.

stretto (It.)
Drawn together, close. (1) Indication to quicken pace. (2) In a **fugue**, the term describes the overlapping of the entries when the subject begins in one voice before the preceding entry has finished. A *stretto maestrale* occurs when an entire entry is subject to overlapping.

strich (Ger.)
A bow stroke.

stringendo (It., 'tightening')
A heightening of tension in the music which in effect means an increase in speed.

string orchestra
Solely a string band as opposed to a wind or brass brand, normally consisting of first and second violins, violas, 'cellos and double basses.

string quartet
A string group consisting of two violins, viola and 'cello.

stromentato (It.)
Played by instruments. *Recitative stromentato* described the 18th-century expressive style of **recitative** (as used by Bach) accompanied by the orchestra.

strophic
Term describes a song which uses the same music for each verse.

stück (Ger.)
A composition, piece.

study or **étude** (Fr.)
Music designed to improve a specific branch of technique by practice. Chopin and Clementi, however, wrote many of artistic merit.

sturm und drang (Ger., 'storm and stress')
The powerful romantic expressiveness sweeping Austrian and German music in the 1760s and 1770s was so called. Especially evident in Haydn's symphonies of that time.

style galant (Fr.), **galanter stil** (Ger.)
The musical equivalent of the rococo style in painting. The term described the homophonic but ornamented French and Italian music between 1730 and 1770 written by F. Couperin and D. Scarlatti. It contrasted with the German contrapuntal style.

sub-dominant
The name for the fourth degree of the scale, e.g. F in the scale of C major. A *plagal cadence* is achieved by the progression of the sub-dominant chord, e.g. F A C in the key of C, followed by the tonic chord C E G, sounding 'Amen'.

subito (It.)
Suddenly.

subject
A group of notes or a theme forming a basic element or idea in a composition by repetition and development.

sub-mediant
The sixth degree of the scale, e.g. A in the scale of C major. The sub-mediant chord in C major is A C E.

suite (Fr., 'a following')
Commonly describes an instrumental piece in several movements consisting of a sequence of dances. In the 17th and 18th centuries, the suite included the characteristic dance forms **allemande, courante, sarabande** and **gigue**. In the mid-18th century, the **binary form** feature of the dances was developed into sonata form. The sonata and also the symphony then became the chief instrumental forms. In the 19th and 20th centuries the term describes a lighter work than a sonata. A suite

may also describe a set of movements assembled from a ballet or opera score.

suivez (Fr., 'follow')
(1) Go staight on to the next section or movement without a break. (2) An indication to an accompanist to follow any changes in tempo made by the soloist.

sul ponticello (It.)
A bowing indication for string players to play near the bridge to achieve a brittle tone.

sul tasto (It.)
A bowing indication to string players to play near or above the fingerboard, producing a 'colourless' tone.

supertonic
The second degree of the scale, e.g. D in the scale of C major. The supertonic chord in C major is D F A.

sur la touche (Fr.)
Same as **sul tasto**.

suspension
A harmonic device whereby a note in a chord is kept sounding whilst another chord is played forming a discord. This discord is resolved by the prolonged note usually falling (but occasionally rising) to a note forming part of the new chord. If this prolonged note rises, then this process is described as *retardation*. See also **anticipation**.

sustaining pedal
The right-hand pedal on the piano which suspends the action of the dampers allowing the strings to vibrate freely.

symphonia
A Greek word taken into Latin and sometimes used in modern contexts to describe a work equivalent to a symphony, e.g. *Symphonia Domestica* written in 1904 by R. Strauss.

symphonic poem
Also known as *programme music* or *tone poem*, this is a mid-19th-century term introduced by Liszt to describe an orchestral piece

influenced by a non-musical theme, e.g. literature, art, or emotions.

symphony

Generally a four-movement, serious and large-scale sonata-like orchestral work involving a first movement, second movement, minuet and trio and finale. The first movement is often in **sonata form**, and this structure may also be evident in the slow movement and finale. This four-movement form became standard around 1760 with Mozart and Haydn but the number of movements may vary.

syncopation

Emphasis on the off-beat and a characteristic of jazz styles.

T

tablature

The notation in diagrams of guitar chords in pop music. Previously, it represented a method of notation involving symbols denoting the positions of the performer's fingers, e.g. for the lute.

tacet (Lat., 'silent')

An indication that a performer or instrument has no part in a particular movement or section.

tafelmusik (Ger., 'table music')

Music suitable for social gatherings, e.g. for performance after or during a dinner.

talcon (Fr.)

The end of the bow (held by the player).

tango

An Argentinian dance in moderately slow time with syncopated rhythms, appearing in European and US ballrooms around World War I.

tanto (It.)

So much. *Allegro non tanto*, not too fast.

tanz (Ger.)

Dance.

tarantella (It.)

A very fast Italian dance with alternating major and minor key sections in 6/8 time.

tardo (It.)
Slow.

tedesco (It., 'German')
Alla tedesca, in the German fashion, usually implying music to be played in the style of a German dance.

tema (It.)
Theme.

temperament
The system of tuning intervals in order to fit them for practicable performance. The piano, organ and other fixed instruments are tuned to *equal temperament* which means that each semitone is made an equal interval so that, e.g. G sharp and A flat are the same.

tempo (It.)
Time, pace.

temps (Fr.)
Beat.

ten.
Abbreviation of (1) tenor and (2) **tenuto**.

tenendo (It.)
Sustaining.

teneramente (It.)
Tenderly.

tenor
(1) Adult male voice between bass and alto. (2) Part above the bass in a four part vocal composition in S A T B (soprano, alto, tenor, bass). (3) In sacred polyphonic music before 1450, this was the lowest melodic part upon which the composition was based. (4) A prefix to an instrument, e.g. tenor saxophone indicating the size between alto and bass. (5) The tenor clef is the C clef on the fourth line.

tenor clef

tenuto (It.)

A held or sustained note (of a single note or chord) where one might expect to play staccato. Abbreviation is *ten*.

ternary form

A composition in three sections in the form A B A with the first section (A) being repeated (not necessarily exactly). B represents a different middle section.

tessitura (It., 'texture')

The natural compass of a singer's voice, or simply the compass of a vocal or instrumental part in a composition.

theme

A melodic group of notes forming the basis or chief idea in a composition by repetition or development. In musical analysis it is equated with **subject**. The term *theme and variations* describes a long musical statement which is developed.

thorough bass

Same as **continuo**.

tie

In musical notation this is a line joining two adjacent notes of the same pitch together, indicating that the first note only should be played but should be prolonged until the second note's time value is up.

tierce de picardie or **picardie third**

This is the surprise sounding of a major third as the final chord in a piece otherwise in the minor key. Common up to the mid-18th century.

time

This describes the basic rhythmical patterns in music, e.g. 6/8 time or common time(4/4). Also march time, waltz time etc.

time signature

The sign of figures at the beginning of a composition or section or movement indicating the number and kind of beats to the bar, e.g. 3/4 indicates 3 crotchet beats to the bar, with the number 4 signifying that the basic beat is a crotchet.

tiré (Fr., 'pulled')
See **down-bow**.

toccata (from Italian *toccare*, 'to touch')
Generally a solo instrumental piece involving rapid changes of notes to demonstrate the player's touch. Often the toccata is followed by a **fugue**, e.g. Bach's famous *Toccata and Fugue in D minor*.

ton (Fr.)
In various contexts this term may mean either note, tone or key.

ton (Ger.)
Note or sound (not the interval of a tone, i.e. two semitones). *Tonreih*, note row.

tonada (Sp.)
Tune, air. *Tonadilla*, Spanish stage entertainment involving a few singers.

tonal answer
In a fugue, for example, after the first entry has been stated there is an answer (or second statement at a different pitch). If this answer is slightly modified to keep the music within a certain key, then this is a tonal answer and the fugue a tonal fugue. This is the opposite of **real answer**.

tonality
Observance of a single key. *Atonality*, lack of key. *Polytonality*, the simultaneous use of several keys.

tone

(1) The interval consisting of two semitones, e.g. C to D is one whole tone. (2) The quality of sound, e.g. in the phrase 'a good tone'. (3) Tone-row or twelve-tone referring to **serial** or twelve-note music.

tone cluster

A 20th-century concept of playing an adjacent group of notes on a piano simultaneously by applying the forearm, fist or piece of wood to the keyboard.

tone-colour, timbre (Fr.), **klangfarbe** (Ger.)

This is the characteristic quality of an instrument's or voice's tone. In basic terms it is the quality which distinguishes a note performed on one instrument compared with the same note sounded on an other instrument or sung by a voice. The tone-colour of an instrument corresponds with the harmonics of that instrument.

tone poem

Same as **symphonic poem**.

tone-row

American term for **note-row**.

tonic

The first degree or key-note of the scale, e.g. C in the key of C major or minor.

tonic sol-fa

See **sol-fa**.

tosto (It.)

Quick, rapid.

tranquillo (It.)

Calm.

transition

(1) A subordinate passage serving as a link to another more important one. (2) A sudden change of key not going through the normal procedures referred to as *modulation*.

transposition
   The writing down or performing of music in a different key from the original. Transposing instruments are those which produce different notes from the written notes, and their parts must be transposed accordingly.

traurig (Ger.)
   Sad.

treble
   (1) Treble clef. G clef on the second line. (2) The highest voice in a boys' choir. **Soprano** is used otherwise. (3) The prefix to an instrument of high pitch within a family, e.g. treble recorder.

treble clef

tre corde (It.)
   Indication to pianists that the left-hand pedal is to be released. Also *tutte le corde*.

tremblement (Fr.)
   Trill.

tremolando (It., 'trembling')
   Employing **tremolo**.

tremolo (It.)
   (1) The rapid reiteration of a single note. (2) The alteration of two or more notes.

tremulant
   Organ device of producing a **vibrato** effect by alternately increasing and decreasing the wind pressure.

trepak
   A lively Cossack dance in 2/4 time.

triad
   A three-note chord, e.g. C E G with E and G being a third and fifth above the lowest note C. An *augmented* triad contains the augmented fifth, e.g. C E G sharp. A *diminished* triad is C E flat G flat.

113

trill

A musical ornament consisting of rapid alternation starting with the written note and then the note above. In the 17th and 18th centuries the trill started with the note above and then the note below. Also known as **shake**.

trinklied (Ger.)

Drinking song.

trio

(1) A vocal or instrumental piece for three performers, e.g. a piano trio (piano, violin and 'cello) and string trio (violin, viola and 'cello). (2) The middle section of a minuet or scherzo. Originally this was written in three-part harmony and the title remained.

trio sonata

A composition usually for two violins and a 'cello, with a keyboard playing the bass line and supporting harmonies. Much favoured in the late 17th and early 18th centuries.

triple concerto

A **concerto** for three solo instruments with orchestra.

triple counterpoint

Invertible counterpoint in which three parts can be interchanged, each making a suitable bass for the other.

triple stop

The playing of three notes simultaneously on a stringed instrument by the placing of the left-hand fingers on the strings and shortening the vibrating length.

triplet

A group of three notes played in the time of 2.

triple time

Time consisting of three beats to the bar, e.g. 3/4, 3/2, 3/8.

triple tonguing
> The rapid articulation of T-K-T on a wind instrument. This is difficult to achieve on reed instruments.

tritone
> The interval of three tones, e.g. F to B.

tronco (It., 'truncated')
> A note broken off abruptly especially in vocal music.

troppo (It.)
> Too much. *Allegro non troppo*, fast but not too fast.

tuning
> See **temperament**.

turca, alla (It.)
> In the Turkish style.

turn
> A musical ornament turning around a note starting with the note above.

tutte le corde (It.)
> Indication to pianist to release the left-hand pedal.

tutti (It.)
> Generally this term means 'all the players', e.g. in a concerto, the expression is used when the orchestra is playing without the soloist. In choral works tutti means chorus as opposed to soloists, or full chorus as opposed to semi-chorus.

twelve note
> See **serial music**.

twelve tone
> American term for **serial music**.

U

über (Ger.)
Over, above.

übung (Ger.)
Exercise. *Clavierübung*, keyboard exercise.

umkehrung (Ger.)
Inversion, reversal.

umore (It.)
Humour. *Con umore*, with humour.

una corda (It.)
Indication to pianists to use the left-hand pedal to reduce the volume.

unison
The sound of two or more voices singing simultaneously at the same pitch. *Unison song*, a song for several people all singing the same tune.

unruhig (Ger.)
Restless.

unter (Ger.)
Under, lower.

upbeat
The upward movement of a conductor's hand or baton, especially indicating the beat before the main accent in a bar of music.

up-bow

A bow stroke on stringed instruments from point to heel. See **bowing** and **down-bow.**

utility music or **gebrauchmusik** (Ger.)

Hindemith's term for works (mainly in the 1920s) intended to be closer to the public and directed to a social or educational purpose, utilising idioms in everyday use. Gebrauchmusik was represented in many forms, including music written to be played by anyone.

V

v
Abbreviation for violin and voice.

valse (Fr.)
Waltz.

vamp
Generally this means to improvise a song accompaniment.

variation
The modification or development of a theme, passage or figure with the theme always remaining recognisable.

vc.
Abbreviation for cello.

verismo (It.)
Realism. Particularly applied to Italian opera around 1900 with its violent and contemporary leanings.

verschiebung (Ger.)
Indication to pianists to use the soft pedal (left-hand pedal).

verse anthem
An **anthem** using the device of one or more solo voices with independent accompaniment for the important parts, contrasted with the full choir.

vibrato
A rapid but minute fluctuation in pitch to give an expressive quality to a note, e.g. by a violinist's oscillations of the left hand. However, this can easily be exaggerated, especially with the voice.

vide (Fr.)
Empty. *Corde à vide*, open string.

vif (Fr.)
Lively.

virtuoso
A performer with brilliant technique and exceptional skill.

vite (Fr.)
Fast.

vivace (It.)
Lively.

vivo (It.)
Lively.

vla
Abbreviation for viola.

vocalise (Fr.)
A wordless composition for performance, e.g. in an opera or as an exercise for solo voice.

voce (It.)
Voice. *Sotto voce*, in a subdued tone.

voice
(1) The sound produced by humans and animals by vibrating the vocal chords. (2) A line or separate strand of music in harmony or counterpoint which is either sung or played, e.g. a fugue in four voices (or four parts).

volante (It.)
Fast and light.

volta (It.)
Time. (1) The terms *prima volta* (first time) and *seconda volta* (second time) are used when a section of a composition, or the composition, is to be repeated with some change in the final bar(s) indicated by these words and horizontal brackets. (2) A

volti

lively dance in 6/8 time popular in the late 16th and early 17th centuries in which men swing women high in the air.

volti (It.)

Turn over (the page) quickly. *Volti subito*, turn quickly.

voluntary

(1) Generally a free-style keyboard piece. (2) An organ solo played before and after an Anglican service.

vorschlag (Ger.)

An **appoggiatura**.

vorspiel (Ger.)

A prelude.

W

waltz
> A slow or fast dance in triple time with the characteristic one beat and one chord in the bar. The waltz became universally popular in the 19th century with Viennese composers.

waltzer (Ger.)
> Waltz.

whole note
> American term for semibreve. See table on page 123.

whole tone
> (1) The interval consisting of two semitones, e.g. C to D. (2) The *whole tone scale* is a scale progressing in whole tones only, instead of partly in whole tones and partly in semitones like the major and minor scales. Whole-tone scales were used by Debussy and others.

wiegenlied (Ger.)
> Cradle song.

wuchtig (Ger.)
> Heavy, weighty.

Y

yodel
> Cheerful singing form found in Switzerland and Austrian Tyrol involving alternation between the natural voice and **falsetto**.

Z

zart (Ger.)
Tender. *Zartheit*, tenderness. *Zärtlich*, tenderly.

zaruela (Sp.)
Spanish traditional stage entertainment with satirical spoken dialogue.

zeitmass (Ger.)
Tempo.

ziemlich (Ger.)
Rather. *Ziemlich langsam*, rather slow.

zingarese, alla (It.)
In the style of gypsy music.

zoppa (It., 'limp')
Term describes music with a prominent **Scotch snap** or syncopation.

zurückhaltend (Ger.)
Holding back, slowing down.

zwischenspiel (Ger.)
An interlude or episode, e.g. in a fugue or rondo.

NAMES OF NOTES AND RESTS

NOTE	REST	BRITISH	AMERICAN
𝅝𝅝	▬	breve	double-whole note
𝅝	▬	semibreve	whole note
𝅗𝅥	▬	minim	half note
𝅘𝅥	𝄾 or ᴾ	crotchet	quarter note
𝅘𝅥𝅮	ᴎ	quaver	eighth note
𝅘𝅥𝅯	ᴎ	semiquaver	sixteenth note
𝅘𝅥𝅰	ᴱ	demisemiquaver	thirty-second note
𝅘𝅥𝅱	ᴱ	hemidemisemiquaver	sixty-fourth note

KEYS and KEY SIGNATURES

MAJOR KEY	RELATIVE MINOR KEY	KEY SIGNATURE (sharp keys)	KEY SIGNATURE (flat keys)
C	A		—
G	E		—
D	B		—
A	F♯		—
E	C♯		—
B = C♭	G♯		
F♯ = G♭	E♭		
C♯ = D♭	B♭		
A♭	F	—	
E♭	C	—	
B♭	G	—	
F	D	—	

125

notes